BUILDING AMERICA
THEN AND NOW

⊨ THE ⊨

BROOKLYN BRIDGE

BUILDING AMERICA: THEN AND NOW

The Alaska Highway

The Brooklyn Bridge

The Eisenhower Interstate System

The Empire State Building

The Hoover Dam

New York City's Central Park

The New York City Subway System

The Telephone: Wiring America

BUILDING AMERICA
THEN AND NOW

THE
BROOKLYN BRIDGE

G. S. PRENTZAS

CHELSEA HOUSE
PUBLISHERS
An imprint of Infobase Publishing

*To NB and MM—For all
the good times in Brooklyn.*

The Brooklyn Bridge

Copyright © 2009 by Infobase Publishing

Chelsea House
An imprint of Infobase Publishing
132 West 31st Street
New York, NY 10001

Library of Congress Cataloging-in-Publication Data
Prentzas, G. S.
   The Brooklyn Bridge / by G.S. Prentzas.
     p. cm. — (Building America: then and now)
   Includes bibliographical references and index.
   ISBN 978-1-60413-073-7 (hardcover : alk. paper)
   1. Brooklyn Bridge (New York, N.Y.)—History—Juvenile literature. I. Title. II. Series.

TG25.N53P74 2009
624.2'3097471—dc22   2008025543

Text design by Annie O'Donnell
Cover design by Ben Peterson

Printed in the United States of America

Bang NMSG 10 9 8 7 6 5 4 3 2 1

This book is printed on acid-free paper.

CONTENTS

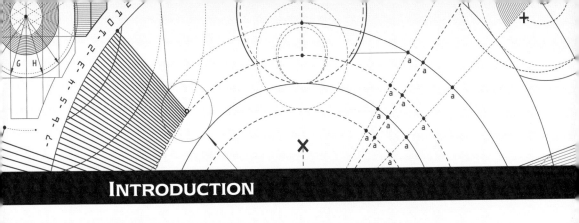

The Eighth Wonder of the World

The Brooklyn Bridge, opened on May 25, 1883, remains one of the world's most recognized structures. At the time, it was hailed as the Eighth Wonder of the World. (The Seven Wonders of the Ancient World were spectacular human-made structures built before 300 B.C. in the vast ancient Greek and Roman empires.) The bridge is widely considered the greatest engineering achievement of the nineteenth century. It stands as a prime example of American technological and architectural progress.

The bridge was built to link New York City and Brooklyn. By the 1860s, many Brooklyn residents worked in New York City. There were no bridges or tunnels at the time, so they had to take ferries across the East River to get to their jobs in New York. The ferries were always crowded, and they were unreliable in bad weather. Brooklyn politicians and businessmen proposed that a bridge be built across the river. It would provide an easy way for people and freight to travel back and forth between Brooklyn and New York.

The Brooklyn Bridge is one of the greatest structures in modern history. Spanning 3,460 feet across the East River in New York City, the bridge has become a famous symbol of the can-do spirit of early America and a young, ambitious metropolis.

The New York state legislature formed a bridge company, a private corporation that would raise money to build the bridge. The company hired John Roebling to design and construct the bridge. Roebling, a brilliant engineer, had developed a successful method for building suspension bridges: He used steel wire cables to support the bridges. Roebling had recently built the world's longest bridge in Cincinnati, Ohio. This renowned engineer and bridge builder accepted the challenge to build a bridge over the turbulent waters of the East River.

Construction on the Brooklyn Bridge began in 1869. The bridge took 14 years to build and cost more than $15 million (about $311 million today), making it the most expensive thing that had ever been built. It also cost the lives of 21 men, including John Roebling. Workers endured dangerous and dreadful working conditions. A mysterious disease struck workmen who dug the bridge's underwater foundations. This disease injured Washington Roebling, who took charge of the project following his father's death. The younger Roebling suffered from the disease throughout the construction of the bridge.

When it was completed, the Brooklyn Bridge was an engineering marvel, larger than any other structure on Earth. It was the world's longest bridge—50 percent longer than its closest rival. Its towers soared nearly seven times higher than New York's tallest buildings. It was the world's first modern bridge, built using new techniques that are still employed today. The Brooklyn Bridge was the first suspension bridge to be constructed of steel, the first bridge to be coated with the metal zinc to protect it from rust, and the first bridge to be illuminated by electric lights.

Because of its engineering innovations, architectural beauty, and spectacular location overlooking New York and its harbor, the bridge came to represent larger ideas. It was the first symbol of modern New York. Within 50 years, hundreds of steel skyscrapers would be built in New York that would stand much taller than the Brooklyn Bridge. Cars would replace horse carriages as the vehicles that crowded the bridge's roadway.

On a larger scale, the Brooklyn Bridge became a shining symbol of the United States in the years following the Civil War (1861–1865). In that era, Americans believed that people could overcome almost any obstacle. While the bridge was being built, the nation experienced an explosion of technological and economic progress. The 1869 joining of the Central Pacific and Union Pacific railways created the nation's first transcontinental railroad. Alexander Graham Bell patented the telephone in 1876. Three years later, Thomas Edison invented the incandescent lightbulb. In 1888, five years after the bridge opened, George Eastman introduced Kodak cameras, which allowed anyone to take photographs.

The Brooklyn Bridge was the crowning achievement of late-nineteenth-century America. The bridge showcased new advances in science and engineering, and it displayed the eagerness

BRIDGE BASICS

Nature created the first bridges, which were rock spans carved out by water running beneath them. The first bridges made by humans were constructed of wood or stone: A dead tree trunk was placed across a stream, for example, or rocks were stacked together to make a simple archway across a gorge.

To work without collapsing, a bridge has to hold up to a combination of three things: its dead load, its live load, and its environmental load. A bridge's own weight makes up its dead load. People, cars, trucks, and other types of traffic passing over the bridge are its live load. External forces—such as water, wind, or earthquakes—constitute a bridge's environmental load. Bridge designers make sure that their bridges can hold up to these three types of loads.

Modern bridges use the characteristics of their building materials to overcome the physical forces that affect them. Four different types of physical forces affect a bridge: tension, compression, torsion, and shear. Tension pulls bridge materials apart; compression pushes bridge materials together; torsion twists bridge materials; and shear breaks off bridge materials.

Bridge builders use materials that will hold up to the pressures exerted by those four forces. Stones have good strength against compression (they hold up heavy weights) but not much strength against tension (they are easy to pull apart). Wood holds up well to both compression and tension, but it is vulnerable to rot, insects, and fire. Ropes and wire cables have good strength against tension (they hold up against pulling) but little strength against compression (they cannot support much weight). In the nineteenth century, bridge builders used iron and steel because they stood up against all four types of forces. In the twentieth century, bridge builders began to use reinforced concrete because it is very strong against compression and tension.

of Americans to attempt things that previously seemed beyond the reach of humans. John Roebling captured the attitude of the times. In the plans he submitted to the bridge company, he declared:

> The present age is emphatically an age of usefulness. . . . No matter what may be charged against the material tendencies of the present age, it is through material advancements alone that a higher spiritual culture of the masses can be attained. The rich gifts of nature must first be rendered subservient [obedient] to man before he can hope to comprehend her true spirit. In this sense the advancement of the sciences and various arts of life may well be hailed as the harbingers [messengers] of good. . . . The works of industry will be sown broadcast over the surface of the earth, and want will disappear.

More than 120 years later, the Brooklyn Bridge's importance lives on. It continues to show that Americans can achieve the impossible.

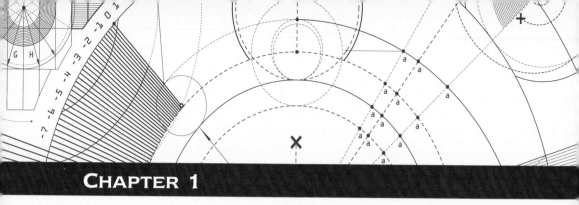

CHAPTER 1

A City of Islands

When most people think of New York City today, they picture skyscrapers, crowded sidewalks, and the bright lights of Times Square. Home to more than 8.2 million people, it is the most populous city in the United States. The New York City metropolitan area has a population of nearly 22 million and includes parts of southern Connecticut, southern New York State and eastern Long Island, and northern New Jersey; it is the third most populous metropolitan area in the world. (Only the Tokyo and Mexico City metropolitan areas have more people.) New York City is the nation's center of business, media, art, and fashion. It attracts tourists from around the world.

New York City consists of five boroughs, or townships: Manhattan, Brooklyn, Queens, Staten Island, and the Bronx. Manhattan and Staten Island are islands. Brooklyn and Queens are located on the western end of another island, Long Island. (Long Island is appropriately named: It stretches 118 miles [190 km] east from New York Bay.) Located at the southern tip of New

York State, the Bronx is the only borough located on the U.S. mainland.

Today, 19 bridges span New York City's many waterways. Along with six tunnels and several ferry lines, these bridges have a very important job: They connect the five boroughs to one another and to the mainland. Traveling across New York City's many waterways, however, has not always been so easy.

WATER EVERYWHERE

Most of New York City's natural features were created about 10,000 years ago. During the last ice age (70,000 to 10,000 years ago), large sheets of ice, known as glaciers, pushed south from what is now Canada. They reached as far south as present-day New York City. About 10,000 years ago, the world's climate became warmer, which caused the thick, heavy ice sheets to melt. As the glaciers slowly retreated north, they scraped out valleys and dragged along boulders, sand, and soil. All that water dripping from melting glaciers caused sea levels to rise.

Some of these valleys filled with water and created new waterways in what is now New York City. One long gorge stretched

THE CONSOLIDATION OF NEW YORK CITY

New York City, as we know it today, did not exist until 1898. Before then, when someone said "New York City," they were referring to Manhattan. On January 1, 1898, Manhattan, the Bronx, Brooklyn, Queens, and Staten Island (then known as Richmond) united to form the City of New York. Four years earlier, the residents of these five cities voted on whether to unite. The measure had passed by a vote of 176,170 to 131,706. The vote had been very close in Brooklyn, with only 300 more "yes" votes than "no." The consolidation of New York City created a city of 3.35 million people.

After the ancient glaciers had melted over New York City, there were bodies of water all over what are now the five boroughs. In this bird's-eye view of Manhattan, the Hudson River *(left)* and the East River *(right)* separate the borough from New Jersey and Brooklyn.

325 miles (456 km) south from the Adirondack Mountains in northern New York State to New York Bay—it became a broad river, now known as the Hudson River. A deep, wide basin formed at the mouth of this river; this basin is now known as New York Bay. The shallow valley carved out along the north side of Long Island filled with seawater; this is now called the Long Island Sound. Shallow ravines east and north of Manhattan also filled with seawater; they are now known as the East River and the Harlem River, respectively.

The glaciers left behind about 770 miles (1,239 km) of waterfront in New York City. The Hudson River runs along the west side of Manhattan and forms the border with New Jersey. On the east side of Manhattan, the East River separates Manhattan from Brooklyn and Queens. Farther northwest, the East River divides the Bronx from Queens. The East River is not actually a river—it is a saltwater strait, or channel. It flows between Long Island Sound and Upper New York Bay. The Harlem River is also a saltwater strait. It connects the East River with the Hudson River, and it separates Manhattan from the Bronx.

THE FIRST NEW YORKERS

Soon after the glaciers retreated, wildlife moved into the New York City region. Woolly mammoths, bison, bears, and giant beavers were among the large animals that roamed the area in search of food. Small bands of nomadic people soon arrived, tracking and hunting these animals. Scientists believe that the ancestors of these hunters had found their way to North America by walking over a land bridge between Asia and Alaska. The land bridge was exposed when sea levels were much lower than now because glaciers still held so much of the world's water. This land bridge is now under the shallow waters of the Bering Sea, located between Alaska and Russia. The descendants of these hunters spread out all over the Americas. In the New York City area, they left evidence of their presence in the form of flint spear points and mounds of discarded animal bones. These first New Yorkers left the region when the animals that they hunted moved north because of increasing temperatures.

About 6,500 years ago, people returned to the New York City area and set up camp around the mouth of the Hudson River. These groups lived off of the abundant animal and plant life of the region's forests and waterways. They fed themselves by hunting deer, wild turkey, and rabbits as well as other small mammals. They fished in the rivers and harbor, and they collected oysters, clams, and other shellfish. They also gathered nuts, berries, and plants.

By the time Europeans first arrived at the mouth of the Hudson River in 1524, the region was inhabited by as many as 15,000 people. Most of these people spoke Munsee, a dialect of the Delaware language. They called themselves the Lenni Lenape. Other groups of Native Americans—including the Raritans, Hackensacks, Tappens, Canarsies, and Rockaways—lived in nearby parts of Connecticut, lower New York State, New Jersey, and Long Island.

The region's native peoples lived in bands that camped in different places, depending on the season. In the spring, they planted corn, beans, squash, tobacco, and other crops on inland fields. During the summer, they camped near the water, where they fished and gathered shellfish. In the fall, they moved back to their fields to harvest crops. In the winter, they camped in forests, where they could gather firewood, take shelter from foul weather, and hunt. Archeologists (scientists who study the remains of past human societies) have unearthed about 80 Lenape campsites in New York City.

Lenape women did most of the farmwork. They planted seeds, tended and harvested the crops, and dried food for storage. They also took care of children and cooked meals. Men hunted and fished. They also built temporary shelters at the seasonal camp-sites. The Lenape had few personal possessions; they owned mostly tools, clothing, and food storage containers. By the six-teenth century, the island of Mannahatta, as the Lenape called it, had no permanent residents.

EUROPEANS ARRIVE

The first Europeans known to have arrived in what is now New York City were the men aboard the French ship *La Dauphine*. King Francis I of France had sent the vessel to find a northern shipping route to China and Japan. French merchants wanted a quicker way to ship silk, spices, and other goods from Asia to Europe. Italian navigator Giovanni da Verrazzano (c. 1485–1528) was the ship's captain. Verrazzano and his crew first sighted North America off the coast of present-day South Carolina. From there, they sailed north. They entered Lower New York Bay in April 1524. The ship dropped anchor at a point between Staten Island and Brooklyn now known as the Narrows. (It anchored near the present location of the Verrazano-Narrows Bridge.) A group of Lenape paddled their boats out to greet the foreigners.

"The people," Verrazzano later wrote in his account of the voyage, "clothed with the feathers of various colors, came toward us joyfully, shouting with admiration, showing us where we could land the boat more safely." Verrazzano could see Upper New York Bay, but he mistook it for a lake. With a storm fast approaching, he decided not to explore the area; the ship hauled anchor. Verrazzano and his crew continued north along the coastline. They sailed along the coast all the way to Newfoundland before returning to France.

One year later, the Spanish ship *La Anunciada* sailed into New York Bay. Spain's King Charles I had hired Portuguese captain Esteban Gómez (c. 1483–1538) to find a western route to the Pacific Ocean. Charles sought to improve his country's trade with the Spice Islands (now Indonesia). Gómez sailed up the Hudson River but quickly turned around. He continued to explore the eastern coast of North America before returning to Spain. More than 80 years passed before another European ship arrived in New York Bay.

THE VERRAZANO-NARROWS BRIDGE

Named after Giovanni da Verrazzano, the Verrazano-Narrows Bridge connects Brooklyn with Staten Island. When it opened in 1964, the Verrazano-Narrows Bridge (notice that one of the z's was mistakenly omitted) was the world's longest suspension bridge. It stretches 7,200 feet (2,195 m) and has a center span (the distance between its two towers) of 4,260 feet (1,298 m). Its 693-foot (211-m) towers are 1.625 inches (4.13 cm) farther apart at their tops. Because the bridge's center span measures nearly a mile, the builders had to compensate for the Earth's curvature. The bridge's cables contain enough wire to circle the Earth more than five times! When completed, the Verrazano-Narrows Bridge was the world's heaviest bridge. It was built to carry a large volume of traffic—today, nearly 200,000 vehicles cross the bridge every day.

DUTCH NEW YORK

In 1609, the *Halve Maen* (*Half Moon*), a small Dutch ship under the command of Englishman Henry Hudson (c. 1565–1611), sailed into New York Bay. Like Verrazzano and Gómez, Hudson had been hired to search for a water route that connected the Atlantic and Pacific oceans. Hudson sailed north up the river (later named after him) to present-day Albany. He turned around when the river became too shallow to continue. Hudson returned to Europe and claimed the New York City area and the Hudson River Valley for the Netherlands.

The Dutch government granted the West India Company the right to oversee its new colony in North America. In 1624, 30 Dutch families arrived in present-day Manhattan. These colonists made a living trading furs with local Indians. Furs were a luxury good in Europe; beaver furs, prized for their softness and water-repellent qualities, were used to make fashionable hats for men. Beaver fur was also thought to cure toothaches, stomachaches, and even poor vision.

In 1626, Peter Minuit (1580–1638), the new general director of the Dutch West India Company, arrived. According to legend, he traded beads, tools, and other goods worth 60 guilders (about 24 dollars) to the Lenape in exchange for the island of Manhattan. (Many historians think that the Lenape believed they were renting the land to the Dutch, not selling it.) Minuit changed the name of Manhattan Island to New Amsterdam (after the Dutch capital). The Dutch colony, called New Netherlands, spread up the Hudson River. Colonists set up farms and trading posts. The Dutch who settled in the farming village on the western tip of Long Island named their new town after the Dutch city of Breuckelen. It is now known as Brooklyn.

Under the leadership of Minuit's successor, Peter Stuyvesant (c. 1612–1672), New Amsterdam soon became an important trading port. New York Bay was an excellent natural harbor. It was large and deep and provided ships a good place to seek shelter from storms. The city's population grew slowly, from 2,000 in

1655 to nearly 9,000 in 1664. Despite its small size, the colony's farming and fur trade produced much wealth for the colonists and the West India Company. New Netherlands' heyday, however, lasted only a few decades. In 1664, another European country, England, also claimed much of eastern North America as its own. England's King Charles II granted his brother, James, Duke of York, all the land between the Connecticut and Delaware rivers for colonization. This territory included New Netherlands, as well as the homelands of many Native American groups. The Duke of York sent a small fleet of warships to New Amsterdam to seize his claim. Without a navy or army to defend the colony, Stuyvesant reluctantly surrendered New Netherlands to the English on September 9, 1664.

A PROSPEROUS COLONY

The British changed the name of New Amsterdam to New York, in honor of the Duke of York. The residents quickly adjusted to English rule, and the city became a vital part of England's colonial empire. Through its seaport, merchants shipped agricultural products from North America to England and to England's Caribbean colonies. England particularly prized Jamaica and other Caribbean colonies because they produced sugar, a very profitable crop.

Throughout the eighteenth century, New York City expanded as a commercial, political, and cultural center; however, it did not yet rival Boston or Philadelphia, the two biggest cities in the colonies. New York's first newspaper, the *Gazette*, began publication in 1725. The city's first college, Kings College (now Columbia University), opened its doors in 1754. Successful merchants and wealthy landowners from the Hudson Valley and Long Island built posh homes in the city.

New York City also served as a command center for military operations against two distinct threats to England's colonies: Native Americans and France. As more and more English settlers intruded on Indian territories along the East Coast, tensions between Native Americans and colonists grew. Indian raids on settlers became more frequent. In response, England began providing troops to defend frontier villages. At the same time, the French also claimed a vast territory in North America. It stretched from eastern Canada west to Minnesota and south to Louisiana, and included western New York State. England viewed the French presence as an obstacle to the expansion of its North American colonies.

Tensions also grew between England and it colonies. England passed laws to tax the colonists to help pay for the troops stationed in North America. The colonists were outraged by these taxes because they had no representation in the English legislature. In 1770, British troops killed five colonists during a confrontation between troops and citizens in Boston. Three years later, colonists destroyed British tea shipments during the Boston Tea Party. Throughout the colonies, people began thinking that the colonies should free themselves from England.

The disagreements finally boiled over in April 1775. The British commander in Boston sent troops to nearby Concord, Massachusetts, to seize weapons and arrest leaders of the rebellion movement. During the Battle of Lexington and Concord, British troops killed eight Massachusetts militiamen. As the army returned to Boston, armed colonists killed 20 British soldiers and wounded about 200 more. This battle marked the beginning of the American Revolution.

INDEPENDENCE

In the spring of 1776, the Continental army began preparing to defend New York City. The rebels predicted that the British would attack the city. If the British controlled New York City and the Hudson River Valley, they could effectively separate New England from the southern colonies. On June 29, an imposing fleet of more than 100 British ships, including 30 battleships, anchored in New York Bay. One American soldier declared, "I thought all of London was afloat."

Five days later, representatives from each of the 13 colonies signed the Declaration of Independence, which proclaimed that the English colonies were now 13 independent states. They had united to defend their freedom. Philip Livingston of Manhattan and Lewis Morris of the Bronx were among the document's signers.

Under the command of General William Howe, the British set up their headquarters on Staten Island. On August 22, an army of 21,000 British soldiers crossed the Narrows and landed in Brooklyn. Five days later, they clashed with the 10,000-man Continental army, under the command of General George Washington. In the early morning hours of August 27, British forces slipped through a gap in the American defenses. Overrun by British troops, the Continental army was quickly routed. During the Battle of Brooklyn, as it became known, the British army killed about 1,200 Americans; approximately 1,500 more Americans were wounded, captured, or listed as missing. The surviving soldiers retreated to Brooklyn Heights.

On the night of August 30, Washington's entire army used sloops, barges, canoes, and any other boat that they could find to make a daring escape across the East River. On September 15, the British easily captured Manhattan. Once again, the Continental army scattered as the British army approached. The Americans retreated north through Manhattan and into the Bronx. Soon after midnight on September 21, a fire started at a tavern in lower Manhattan. Strong winds spread the fire from one building to the next. Fire destroyed more than 500 buildings—about a quarter of the city's structures. The British believed that a rebel arsonist had started the fire. Many New Yorkers were convinced that the British had set the tavern on fire.

The British occupation of New York City lasted throughout the war. The Treaty of Paris was signed in September 1783, ending the American Revolution. Two months later, the remaining British soldiers left the city. Jubilant crowds greeted George Washington as he triumphantly marched into New York City on

November 25, 1783. The U.S. Congress held its first session in the city on March 4, 1789. (Congress moved the federal capital to Philadelphia in 1790 and finally to Washington, D.C., in 1800.) George Washington was inaugurated as the new nation's first president on the balcony of the original city hall on April 30.

THE RISE OF A GREAT CITY

Following the revolution, New York City grew as the nation's economic center, particularly after the opening of the Erie Canal in 1825. The canal was the greatest engineering feat of its time: It was 363 miles (584 km) long, 40 feet (12 m) wide, and 4 feet (1.2 m) deep. It featured 83 locks, mechanisms that raised or lowered boats so they could pass from a body of water at one level to another situated at a higher or lower level. The Erie Canal connected New York City's harbor to Lake Erie and provided a faster and less expensive east-west transportation route. Settlers and manufactured goods traveled west on the canal. Agricultural goods produced in the Great Lakes region—particularly corn and wheat—were shipped east.

New York City immediately became the link between industrialized European countries and the United States' agricultural frontier. By 1835, New York City surpassed Philadelphia as the country's most populous city; its population grew from 123,706 in 1820 to 942,292 in 1870. The city bristled with commerce. Its stock market, banks, and insurance companies helped businesses across the country grow. Because of its telegraph companies and newspapers, New York became a communications hub. Department stores, shops, hotels, and restaurants opened to serve New Yorkers and visitors alike.

The potato famine of the 1840s in faraway Ireland had a profound impact on New York City. Large numbers of Irish immigrants braved transatlantic voyages to start a new life in the United States. By 1850, Irish immigrants made up one-quarter of the city's population. By employing the labor of these new

The largest battle of the American Revolution took place in Brooklyn. *Above,* George Washington and officers of the victorious Continental army ride into New York City after the war's end.

residents, New York soon became the nation's largest manufacturing center.

Across the East River, Brooklyn experienced a similar expansion. The Dutch had first settled on the western tip of Long Island in 1634. Their first village was Midwout (now Midwood), and two years later the Dutch West India Company established the village of Brueckelen. After the British seized control of New Netherlands, the name of the village eventually changed to its current form: Brooklyn.

Until the early nineteenth century, Brooklyn looked much like it did during Dutch colonial days. It remained mostly rural, and its population did not reach 5,000 until 1800. The economic growth spurred by the opening of the Erie Canal changed Brooklyn forever. Because of the deeper waters of the East River along its shore, the Brooklyn waterfront began to rival Manhattan as a shipping center. Shipbuilding companies set up large shipyards on the Brooklyn side of the river. Brooklyn factories manufactured glass, steel, hats, chemicals, glue, and other products. By 1860, its population approached 400,000, making it the third most populous U.S. city (though it still had less than half the population of Manhattan).

In 1861, the Confederate states seceded, or separated, from the United States. Two hundred and fifty thousand people crowded into Union Square to show their support for the Union. Two years later, however, more than 15,000 men devastated the city during a weeklong rampage known as the Draft Riot. These men were protesting the enactment of the nation's first-ever military draft. The Union army had to quell the riot. More than 100 people were killed, making it the most deadly episode of civil disorder in U.S. history. In April 1865, news of the assassination of President Abraham Lincoln cut short the city's celebration of the Union victory in the Civil War. Thousands of residents lined the streets of Manhattan to view Lincoln's funeral procession, which stopped in New York City on its way to Illinois.

CROSSING THE EAST RIVER

Despite the turmoil of the Civil War, commerce between New York City and Brooklyn remained robust. As a result of the massive influx of immigrants and other newcomers, New York City had become very crowded, expensive, and crime ridden. Many Manhattan residents looked down on Brooklyn as a backwater, but its lower taxes, better schools, safer streets, and good drinking water nonetheless attracted many new residents.

Despite the closeness of the two major cities, a major obstruction still kept them apart: the East River. The turbulent waters of the 16-mile-long (26-km) saltwater strait are notorious. Ocean

In order to meet the needs of the growing populations of Brooklyn and New York, ferry and boat services shuttled people from one side of the East River (*above*) to the other. River traffic and bad weather made these methods less than ideal, however, prompting officials to consider construction projects for tunnels and bridges.

tides push and pull water through the channel, creating unpredictable currents that make boat travel tricky. Dutch sailors named a spot near the river's midway point Helegat ("bright passage"). Because of its dangerous whirlpools and rock outcroppings, English sailors started to call it Hell Gate. As Brooklyn grew, small sailboats and rowboats carried passengers across the half-mile (0.8-km) river. Later, large ferries—and eventually steam ferries—shuttled people and goods back and forth across the treacherous water. By the end of the Civil War, one-third of Brooklyn's workforce commuted to jobs in Manhattan. Five different ferry lines, all operated by Union Ferry Company, steamed back and forth across the East River. They cruised the waters day and night, and made a total of about 1,000 crossings a day. The ferry stations in Manhattan and Brooklyn were crowded with businessmen, laborers, clerks, and delivery boys around the clock.

On good days, the overcrowded ferries were merely annoying. On bad days, they could be deadly. In foul weather, the ferries bobbed crazily in choppy waters. Passengers occasionally were tossed overboard. In dense fogs, boats crashed into each other. In winter, ferries got stuck in ice, causing service cancellations or even stranding passengers midriver. Since 1800, there had

BUILDING AMERICA NOW

EAST SPAN, SAN FRANCISCO– OAKLAND BAY BRIDGE

On October 17, 1989, an earthquake caused part of the San Francisco–Oakland Bay Bridge to collapse. A 50-foot (15-m) section of the upper roadway fell onto the lower roadway. The bridge, which opened in 1936, spans San Francisco Bay and connects two major California cities, San Francisco and Oakland. Crews repaired the bridge, but California Department of Transportation engineers determined that the bridge's eastern span should be replaced. Seeking the best bridge design possible, state officials held an international design competition. A self-anchored suspension bridge featuring a single tower was selected as the winner of the competition. (The cables of a self-anchored suspension bridge are connected to the roadway deck rather than anchored into the ground, as with most suspension bridges.)

When the designers planned the construction of the new East Span, they faced problems similar to those that the designer of the bridge across New York's East River had to overcome more than a century earlier. The bridge would be long (2.8 miles; 4.5 km), had to take into account natural obstacles (including high winds, difficult underwater terrain, saltwater), and could not block boat traffic. Most important, been talk of linking New York City and Brooklyn with a bridge. Engineering knowledge, however, had not advanced far enough to make such a bridge possible. Some experts believed that building a tunnel between the two cities or constructing a dam on the East River made more sense.

The harsh winter of 1866–1867, however, spurred the drive toward making a bridge spanning the East River a reality. That winter was as severe as any on record. The ice conditions on

the bridge across the bay would have to be able to withstand a major earthquake.

Because of the geography of San Francisco Bay and other factors, the new East Span will be a combination of bridges:

1. A short, low-rise bridge connecting the Oakland shore to the main bridge;
2. A 1.5-mile (2.4-km) roadway deck from the low-rise bridge to the suspension bridge;
3. The single-tower, self-anchored suspension bridge; and
4. A roadway deck connecting the suspension bridge to Yerba Buena Island (the Bay Bridge's western span links the island to San Francisco).

When it is finished, the new East Span will be the world's largest single-tower, self-anchored suspension bridge. To withstand earthquakes, it will include several state-of-the-art safety features, such as a shock-absorbing hinge system built into the bridge deck. The new East Span is expected to open by 2013 at an estimated cost of $1.43 billion. A California government spokesman remarked, "All great bridges set new standards for innovation. We are hoping that this bridge does the same."

the East River were the worst ever experienced. Ferries did not operate for days at a time. Brooklyn residents could not get to work in Manhattan. Goods could not travel between the two cities. Fed up with the hassles and unpredictability of the ferries, many people in Brooklyn began to clamor for a bridge. People on both sides of the river saw the advantages that a bridge would bring: It would allow people and products to cross the East River quickly, no matter the weather. A bridge would also help solve Manhattan's overcrowding problem. It would stimulate Brooklyn's growth. Brooklyn business leaders and politicians began working to authorize the construction of a bridge.

CHAPTER 2

A Vision of the Bridge

O n April 16, 1867, the New York legislature passed a bill that created the New York Bridge Company. It would sell stocks (titles to a share in the ownership of a company) to raise money to build a bridge between New York and Brooklyn. Brooklyn's leading politicians and businessmen supported the plan to build a bridge. A former Brooklyn mayor, Henry Murphy, wrote the bill that created the company. Behind the scenes, businessman William Kingsley convinced other business leaders that the bridge needed to be built. The successful 34-year-old contractor had paved many of Brooklyn's streets, installed most of its sewers, and built several of its parks. He also had interests in banks, real estate firms, and other Brooklyn businesses.

The bridge company's board of directors elected Murphy as the company's president. They also appointed John Roebling of Trenton, New Jersey, as the project's chief engineer. Roebling had just finished building the world's longest suspension bridge in Cincinnati and was considered the country's foremost bridge builder. Roebling was the only engineer that the bridge company considered for the job.

THE MASTER BUILDER

John Roebling had led an amazing life. He was born on June 12, 1806, in the ancient walled town of Mühlhausen, Prussia (now Germany). His father, Christoph, owned a tobacco shop. His mother, Friederike, had high hopes for her children. Recognizing John's intelligence early on, she saved money for his education. At age 17, John enrolled in the prestigious Polytechnic Institute of Berlin. He studied engineering and architecture, and received a degree in civil engineering in 1826. (Civil engineering is a branch of engineering concerned with the design and construction of public works, such as dams, highways, and bridges.) The young engineer took a job building roads for the Prussian government. He saw his first suspension bridge in Bamberg, Bavaria (now Germany). The local people called the small chain bridge spanning the Rednitz River the "miracle bridge." Roebling sketched the bridge and wrote an article on its engineering principles. His family later believed that this was the moment when he decided to become a bridge builder.

In 1831, Roebling returned to Mühlhausen. He had decided to organize a group of townspeople to leave their country. In college, Roebling had studied under the famed philosopher Georg Hegel (1770–1831), who had encouraged his best students to move to the United States. In his book *History of Philosophy* (1837), he referred to the young nation as "the land of desire for all those who are weary of the historical lumber room [storeroom] of old Europe." Like many talented Prussians, Roebling did not have very good political or social connections. In Prussia, at that time, most of the best jobs went to members of wealthy or socially prominent families—thus, Roebling found it difficult to get a good job. Taking his professor's advice, he decided to move to the United States. There, he would set up a new community that would give him and his neighbors the chance to reach their potential.

On May 11, 1831, Roebling left town with his brother Karl and 53 men, women, and children. He wrote in his journal, "It is not contempt for our Fatherland that causes us to leave it. . . . It was an inclination and an ardent desire that our circumstances be bettered." Roebling believed that it was his destiny to be an American farmer, even though he had never farmed before. After boarding the ship that carried him across the Atlantic Ocean, he never returned to Europe.

Roebling was very different from most European immigrants in the 1830s. He was not seeking religious freedom. He was not escaping poverty. He traveled in the ship's first-class section, where he had a bed to himself. He brought along a trunk full of books. He and his brother had $600 to buy land and farming tools. In his journal, Roebling recorded the ship's 11-week passage. He wrote down details from his talks with the ship's crew about the technical aspects of sailing. He noted the experience of smelling the North American continent before land came into sight.

Roebling's ship landed in Philadelphia. His group soon headed west across Pennsylvania. In Pittsburgh, the Roebling brothers bought 7,000 acres (2,833 hectares) of land in Butler County, near the town of Harmony. The group named their new village Germania and later changed it to Saxonburg. John Roebling laid out the town's first streets. He wrote home, praising the new settlement, and his letters enticed others from Mühlhausen to make the journey to western Pennsylvania.

The early days of Saxonburg were difficult. The soil was poor and the winters were bitter. Only a few of the settlers knew how to farm. The few experienced farmers taught the others how to grow crops. Soon, their hard work paid off. By 1836, Saxonburg was a working town with carpenters, a blacksmith, and a grocer. That year, John married Johanna Herting, the daughter of a Saxonburg farmer.

Roebling had enjoyed the challenge of setting up Saxonburg, but he soon became bored with farming. He later told his oldest son that he had wanted to "employ science to useful purpose." In

German immigrant John Roebling *(above)* utilized his engineering expertise to design and construct aqueducts and suspension bridges in Pennsylvania and Cincinnati. He became well known for his work and was soon contracted to design and build the Brooklyn Bridge.

1837, he accepted an engineering job that took him all over Pennsylvania. Johanna stayed behind in Saxonburg to take care of the children and the farm. As part of his job, Roebling built dams and locks on the Beaver River Canal, and he surveyed a possible railroad route east of Pittsburgh. That same year, Roebling became a citizen of the United States, and his first child, Washington, was born. Roebling was soon promoted to principal assistant to the state of Pennsylvania's chief engineer. Things were going well when tragedy struck the family: Roebling's brother Karl died of heatstroke while working in the fields.

During his work for a canal company, Roebling saw how workers used hemp rope to transport barges over mountains: They pulled the barges up one side of a hill and lowered them down the other side. He saw several accidents in which the 9-inch (23-cm)-thick ropes broke and heavy barges flew down the hill. One accident killed two men. Roebling had the idea to replace the expensive hemp ropes with 1-inch (2.5-cm) ropes made out of wire. He had read about this new technology in a German scientific journal.

Roebling told canal company officials that wire rope would work better than hemp rope. It was stronger and easier to work with, and it would last much longer. The officials were not convinced. They agreed to let Roebling test a wire rope, but he had to pay for the trial run himself. Roebling returned to Saxonburg to make wire rope for the test. He built a simple machine that twisted strands of wire together and then taught local farmers how to use the machine. Roebling's wire rope passed the test. Soon, the canal company and other businesses were using his wire rope. He increased the amount of wire being made; as a result, some Saxonburg farmers became full-time wire makers.

In 1844, Roebling finally got a chance to build a bridge. Fire had destroyed a wooden *aqueduct* that carried a busy canal over the Allegheny River in Pittsburgh. Roebling's aqueduct, completed that same year, was the first structure of its kind. The wire-suspension aqueduct had seven spans, each of which measured 162 feet (49 m) in length. Two 7-inch (18-cm)-thick wire cables supported a large timber flume that was 16.5 feet (5 m) wide and 8.5 feet (2.6 m) deep. The flume could hold 2,000 tons (1,814 metric tons) of water, plus fully loaded barges. Roebling introduced an important innovation: He came up with a new way to anchor bridge cables to the shore. He attached the cables to large chains of iron eyebars, pieces of metal that have holes in each end. The eyebars were embedded in masonry on the shore. He would use this same method in all of his later bridges.

Roebling's first bridge showed that a suspension bridge could support a lot of weight. He had completed the aqueduct in nine months and for less money than planned. Pennsylvania politicians took notice. When a fire reduced half of Pittsburgh to ashes in April 1845, he was hired to replace a destroyed bridge. His suspension bridge, which spanned the Monongahela River, went up quickly and cheaply. Opened in February 1846, the bridge was an amazing 1,500 feet (457 m) long, with two cables that supported its eight 188-foot (57-m) spans. For this bridge, Roebling used a system of diagonal stays, wires that ran from the bridge's towers to its deck. The stays made the bridge stiffer and sturdier.

The Delaware & Hudson Canal Company hired Roebling to build four more aqueducts. He finished the first and longest of these bridges in 1848. The 535-foot (163-m) bridge crossed the Delaware River at Lackawaxen, Pennsylvania. Its four 8.5-inch (21.6-cm)-thick cables, each composed of 2,150 wires, held up four spans. The Lackawaxen aqueduct later became a highway bridge, and it still stands today. It is the oldest suspension bridge in the United States and appears on the National Register of Historic Landmarks. It is also a National Historical Civil Engineering Landmark. Many of the Lackawaxen bridge's key parts—including cables, piers, and anchorages—remain exactly the way Roebling built them.

In 1848, Roebling decided to move his prosperous wire business to Trenton, New Jersey. Trenton was a transportation hub; it had a seaport and offered easy access to railroad lines. Roebling and his family never returned to Saxonburg.

Brilliant, ambitious, and innovative, Roebling seemed to succeed at everything he tried. He was a celebrated bridge builder. He was a businessman who invented all of the machinery in his wire factory. He spoke perfect English, German, and French. He played the piano and flute. Scientific journals published the engineering articles that he wrote. He kept up-to-date on the latest scientific advances. He read the works of poet and philosopher Ralph Waldo Emerson and other intellectuals of the era. He even worked on writing his own book, which was not so modestly titled *Theory of the Universe*.

Roebling's remarkable success and achievements came with a price. He was difficult to get along with. He was stubborn, inflexible, and sure of his own views. He firmly believed that a scientific approach could solve any problem. One of his favorite mottos was, "If one plan won't do, then another must." He was extremely serious—his employees later recalled his piercing stares and gruff scowls. He refused to meet with anyone who was late for an appointment. He believed that water was the best cure for everything and drank huge amounts of it every day. He took scorching hot baths and wrapped himself with cold, dripping wet sheets afterward.

His greatest ambition had been to build grand bridges. By the age of 42, Roebling had reached the top of his profession. He competed with Charles Ellet, a rival bridge builder, for bridge contracts. In 1847, Ellet had been hired to build a railroad bridge near Niagara Falls, New York. The bridge would cross the Niagara River just below the powerful Niagara Falls. It was a very important project: The bridge would connect the U.S. and Canadian railroad systems.

The Niagara project was an engineering nightmare. The bridge would have to span nearly 1,000 feet (305 m). At the time, the longest wooden bridge was 360 feet (110 m) long; the longest stone bridge was 251 feet (76.5 m) long. The roiling waters of the Niagara Gorge meant there was no place to build piers—only a suspension bridge would work. Ellet first built a temporary bridge, which allowed pedestrians and small carriages to cross the gorge. He argued about money with the bridge company, however, and soon abandoned the project. His temporary bridge was dismantled.

The company invited Roebling to submit plans for the bridge and accepted his design. He began to build a suspension bridge across the Niagara River in 1851. The Niagara Bridge, completed in March 1855, was the longest railroad bridge in the world. Its cables measured 10.25 inches (26 cm) in diameter, and 64 stays supported the bridge. Some engineers claimed that it was the greatest engineering feat of the era; other engineers predicted that it would tumble into the Niagara Gorge. Ultimately, the Niagara Bridge was an important engineering milestone. It helped prove Roebling's belief that suspension bridges were reliable when they were designed correctly and built with the right materials.

The success of the Niagara Bridge elevated Roebling to the top of the bridge-building profession. His critics turned out not to be entirely wrong, however. The increasing weight of trains caused more stress on the bridge than Roebling had expected.

EARLY SUSPENSION BRIDGES

Before the success of Roebling's Niagara Bridge, few people trusted suspension bridges. They had earned a bad reputation because so many of them had failed. In 1831, a suspension bridge in England collapsed as soldiers marched across it. Four more suspension bridges built by the same Englishmen fell down. A suspension bridge in Kentucky collapsed as a herd of cattle was being driven across it. In 1854, wind caused Charles Ellet's suspension bridge in Wheeling, West Virginia, to sway; it broke apart and plunged into the Ohio River. Roebling's bridges worked because of his better designs and his use of improved building materials.

The cables had to be renovated and the anchorages reinforced. Metal trusses replaced Roebling's original wooden trusses, and iron towers replaced his original stone towers. By 1897, the bridge had been replaced entirely.

Roebling's next two projects were suspension bridges—one spanned the Ohio River in Cincinnati, and the other crossed the Allegheny River in Pittsburgh. Construction on the Allegheny Bridge began in 1858. When it opened in 1860, it was the first suspension bridge to be built using metal towers. Construction on the Cincinnati Bridge (now called the John A. Roebling Bridge), which would link Cincinnati, Ohio, and Covington, Kentucky, had been started in 1856. The Civil War delayed construction, so Roebling did not finish the bridge until 1866. With a span of 1,057 feet (322 m), it remained the world's longest suspension bridge until 1883 and established Roebling as a master builder of bridges. He had developed the basic principles of modern suspension bridges. When the officials of the New York Bridge Company gathered to decide whom to hire to build their complex, unprecedented bridge, there was only one person to consider.

DESIGNING THE BRIDGE

As Roebling began to design the bridge, he knew that building it would be the greatest engineering challenge he had ever faced. The bridge would stand in a turbulent saltwater channel that was also one of the world's busiest ports; it had to be high enough to allow tall ships to pass underneath. It would be longer than any bridge in the world and had to be strong enough to support a roadway. The roadway would have heavy carriage, foot, and livestock traffic.

Roebling spent three months making the technical drawings. He sent his son Washington to Europe to observe new bridge-building techniques. He had measurements made of the river's depth and mapped out the terrain of the bottom. He determined the best possible place to situate the bridge.

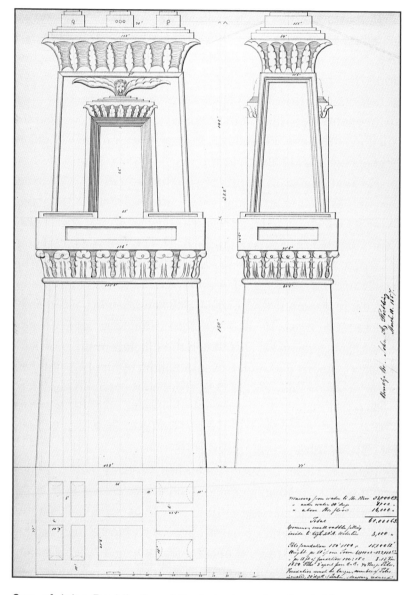

One of John Roebling's original designs for the bridge *(above)* included Egyptian influences, which would have made the structure appear similar to other New York City landmarks, such as the Tombs or the Croton Reservoir. Another Roebling design, featuring neo-Gothic accents, was chosen for the bridge's two stone towers.

In September 1867, Roebling presented his plan to the company's board members. He proposed a suspension bridge with two stone towers located in the water near the New York and Brooklyn shores. The bridge's two roadways would pass through two arches in each tower. Four large 15-inch (38-cm) cables anchored on each shore would hold up the roadways. To allow ships to pass under the bridge, the roadways would be 135 feet (41 m) above the water.

The bridge company accepted Roebling's plan, and excitement about the project grew. It was going to be unlike any other bridge in the world. The two stone towers would be Gothic arches that soared more than 250 feet (76 m) high. The length between the stone towers would be 1,596 feet (486 m; 50 percent longer than Roebling's Cincinnati Bridge). Horses and carriages would use the two outer roadways to cross the bridge, and trains would travel across the inner roadway. The crowning glory of the bridge would be a pedestrian walkway—called a promenade—located above the roadway. People who crossed the bridge on foot would enjoy breathtaking views of New York and its harbor.

Everyone who saw Roebling's sketches knew that the bridge would be beautiful, but some worried that it would not be safe. Two years passed before construction began, because it took that long for the bridge company to raise money by selling stocks. Roebling also had to make early preparations. Meanwhile, critics of the bridge voiced their reservations. Some said that it would cost too much money, and others agreed with *Scientific American* magazine that building a tunnel made more sense. Some engineers even claimed that the bridge could not be built. Behind the scenes, it took great effort to get the bridge approved by the local, state, and federal governments.

Finally, in early 1869, the bridge company had secured all of the government approvals. Roebling could begin to build his bridge. Oddly, the bridge did not have an official name at this time, so Roebling called it the East River Bridge. People in Brooklyn called it the New York Bridge—from their perspective,

BUILDING AMERICA NOW

THE NEW TACOMA NARROWS BRIDGE

The New Tacoma Narrows Bridge opened in July 2007. It spans the Puget Sound between the Washington cities of Tacoma and Gig Harbor. The 5,400-foot (1,646-m) suspension bridge sits beside the existing Tacoma Narrows Bridge (1950). The new bridge, which cost more than $849 million to build, has four lanes for vehicles. It also has a separate, protected lane for pedestrians and bicycles.

The state of Washington built the New Tacoma Narrows Bridge to improve the ability of people and freight to cross the waterway. The extra lanes ease daily traffic jams, and the bridge is designed so that a second deck can be added if bridge usage increases. The new bridge also makes crossing Puget Sound safer. Traffic heading into Tacoma uses the new bridge, whereas traffic leaving the city uses the older bridge. This improves roadway safety by separating the lanes of opposing traffic. The bridge was also designed and built to minimize its effects on the environment. The builders took steps to protect nearby wetlands and to avoid disturbing the underwater ecosystem beneath the bridge.

The Tacoma Narrows is important in bridge-building history. When the original Tacoma Narrows Bridge opened in July 1940, it was the world's third-largest suspension bridge. The slender, graceful bridge soon gained the nickname "Galloping Gertie" because of the way it swayed on windy days. Only four months after it opened, a strong windstorm caused the bridge to start swinging violently. A movie camera captured the bridge breaking apart and plunging into the waters of the sound. Because it was captured on film, Galloping Gertie is perhaps history's most famous bridge failure. Its collapse led to the safer engineering of suspension bridges. Sections of the bridge—now sitting on the bottom of the Puget Sound—have created one of the world's largest human-made reefs. They provide shelter for fish and many other sea creatures.

that was where the bridge went. Likewise, New Yorkers called it the Brooklyn Bridge, which was the name that stuck.

A TERRIBLE ACCIDENT

As Roebling was finishing a survey of sites for the Brooklyn tower, he was injured in a freak accident. On June 28, 1869, John and Washington Roebling were standing on a dock discussing the placement of the bridge towers when a ferry suddenly crashed into the dock. The elder Roebling reacted too slowly, and the boat crushed his right foot against the dock. Doctors amputated his toes, but he stubbornly refused additional medical treatment. Instead Roebling had water poured on the wounds several times a day, and his condition worsened. He contracted tetanus, a horrible and painful infection that affects muscles and tendons. Tetanus, also called lockjaw, causes facial muscles to tighten and freezes the jaw shut. Roebling went into a coma and, on July 22, 1869—only 17 days after the accident—he died.

Some believed that Roebling's death meant the end of the bridge project; however, the following month, the bridge company appointed Washington Roebling as the chief engineer. The 32-year-old had worked on a few of his father's bridges, but he had never built a major suspension bridge by himself. He did,

A TRIBUTE TO JOHN ROEBLING

"One of his strongest moral traits was his power of will, not a will of the stubborn, but a certain spirit, tenacity of purpose, and confident reliance on self . . . an instinctive faith in the resources of his art that no force of circumstance could divert from carrying into effect a project once matured in his mind."

—Charles B. Stuart, an engineer and longtime Roebling friend, in his book *Lives and Works of Civil and Military Engineers of America* (1871)

however, know all there was to know about making the wire cable system of suspension bridges. The decision to hire the young engineer surprised many. More than a few people, including several bridge company officials, doubted that he could finish the project.

IN HIS FATHER'S FOOTSTEPS

Washington Roebling was born on May 26, 1837, in Saxonburg, Pennsylvania. He was John and Johanna's first child. When his family moved to Trenton, the 11-year-old enrolled at the Trenton Academy. While Washington was still a student, he often helped out in the offices of his father's wire factory. In 1854, Washington Roebling began his studies at Rensselaer Polytechnic Institute (RPI). Located in Troy, New York, RPI was considered the nation's best civil engineering school. Its engineering program was difficult, and Roebling had to study hard to keep up with his assignments. For his senior thesis, he designed a suspension aqueduct. Washington graduated in 1857; only 12 of the 65 engineering students in his class received a degree.

Washington returned to Trenton, where he worked at the wire factory for about a year. He then moved to Pittsburgh to help his father build the Allegheny Bridge. When John Roebling left Pittsburgh to start another bridge in Cincinnati, he left Washington in charge of the project. Construction on the Allegheny Bridge ended in 1860, and it was hailed as a success. The bridge was so sturdy that the company that owned it did not even bother to insure it.

In early 1861, Washington Roebling heard Abraham Lincoln give a speech in Trenton. The president's speech motivated the 24-year-old to volunteer for the Union army. With his background as an engineer, Roebling was soon promoted to lieutenant. During the Civil War, he planned bridges and supervised their construction. He designed many different types of bridges. He had to make the designs simple enough that soldiers without bridge-construction experience could build them quickly.

When a tragic accident during bridge construction killed his father, Washington Roebling (*above*) took over the project. Although he had worked with his father as a trained engineer, the Brooklyn Bridge was Washington Roebling's first major construction job without John Roebling. Many doubted that he could finish the bridge.

In 1861, Washington Roebling arrived in Fredericksburg, Maryland, to rebuild a bridge that a flood had destroyed. It would be the first bridge that he built completely on his own. He designed the bridge and served as its engineer and foreman; he also trained the soldiers assigned to him in the basics of bridge building. His crew completed the 1,000-foot (305-m) bridge in two weeks.

In the summer of 1862, Roebling joined the staff of General John Pope. During the war, he took part in several notable battles: the Second Battle of Bull Run, Antietam, South Mountain, and Chancellorsville. In October 1862, he received orders to build a bridge spanning the Potomac River at Harpers Ferry, West Virginia. He finished the bridge in December. In late June 1863, as the Union army retreated toward Gettysburg, Pennsylvania, Roebling went up in a hot-air balloon and provided reports on the positions of the approaching Confederate army. On the second day of the Battle of Gettysburg, Roebling commanded an artillery battalion that defended Little Round Top, a key Union position on the battlefield. Roebling retired from the army on January 1, 1865, with the rank of colonel.

Roebling met his future wife while serving under General Governor Warren. He met Warren's sister, Emily, at an officer's ball. In a letter to his youngest sister, Washington wrote, "It was the first time I ever saw her and I am very much of the opinion that she has captured your brother Washy's heart at last. It was a real attack in force." Emily was the eleventh of twelve children in a family that lived in the small Hudson River town of Cold Spring, New York. Her family was not wealthy, but they were socially prominent. They had ancestors dating back to early colonial days.

Washington and Emily began writing each other daily and eventually married on January 18, 1865. They settled in Trenton, where Washington took charge of the Roebling wire factory. That spring, he traveled to Cincinnati to help his father finish the construction of the Cincinnati Bridge. The couple had a son, whom they named John after Washington's father.

In the summer of 1867, the New York Bridge Company appointed John Roebling as chief engineer of the Brooklyn Bridge. Two years later, when John Roebling died, Washington Roebling was named as his replacement. He was very different from his father: He lacked his father's experience and confidence. Washington was modest, more sociable, and good at dealing with people. He was a great draftsman and an expert at making suspension bridge cables. He wanted to see his father's bridge built, so he accepted the challenge. He noted in his journal that, from that point forward, he would have to rely on himself.

CHAPTER 3

The Towers Go Up

By the autumn of 1889, the New York Bridge Company had sold enough bridge stocks, so officials told Washington Roebling to start building the Brooklyn Bridge. As chief enginer, Roebling had many things to take care of before construction could begin. The Brooklyn Bridge was unlike any other construction project that had ever been built. Roebling hired six young engineers to help him make sure that the bridge was built correctly. Roebling ordered lumber, stone, and other building supplies. He bought air compressors, drills, and other tools. He also began to hire workers—Roebling would eventually be in charge of 1,000 men. He would also have to make every major engineering and construction decision. He would have to consult with the bridge company board of directors, deal with state and local politicians, and ignore the complaints of his critics.

Roebling's first step was to build the bridge's towers. His father had designed two towers to hold up the bridge's huge wire cable suspension system. The towers would sit in the East River, near each shore. They would soar a jaw-dropping 268 feet (88 m) into the air. The bridge's towers would be taller than any other structure in New York or Brooklyn. At the time, the tallest buildings in either of the two cities were only four stories, or less than 60 feet (18 m) tall.

The bottom of the East River did not provide a good, sturdy base for the bridge towers. Layers of mud and soft sand sat at its bottom. Boulders of different sizes also littered the riverbed. To give the towers the strong bases that they needed, Roebling planned to build them on top of sturdy foundations sunk deep into the solid layer of bedrock beneath the river. For these foundations, he would use wooden caissons (French for *box*; pronounced kay-sohn), large boxes with thick roofs and sturdy walls made of wood and iron, but no floor. When pressed down on the river's bottom, a caisson's edges formed a watertight seal. In 1868, Roebling had traveled to Europe, where the use of caissons to build bridge foundations had been invented. He visited several bridge sites to study how the engineers installed and used caissons and then reported his findings to his father. Now he would put that information to use in the construction of the Brooklyn Bridge.

John Roebling's plan called for two 3,000-ton (2,722-metric ton) caissons to be sunk to the bottom of the East River. Workmen would then enter the underwater chamber to remove mud, sand, rocks, and other debris from the riverbed. This would be the most difficult and dangerous part of the bridge's construction. Meanwhile, stonemasons would start building the tower on the caisson's roof.

The caisson would slowly sink as the debris underneath it was removed. The increasing weight of the rising stone towers would also push the caisson's V-shaped bottom edges downward. The tower was built up just enough to keep the top of the structure above water. Eventually, the caisson would strike solid bedrock underneath the river. No one knew how deep workers would have to sink the caisson before it came to rest on bedrock.

Because the bottom of the East River was filled with sand and debris, Washington Roebling devised an underwater method to excavate all unwanted material from his building site. His solution was to use caissons *(above)*—large, watertight chambers that were sunk to the bottom of the river. Men inside would remove large rocks and buckets of muddy sand until they hit solid bedrock.

THE BROOKLYN CAISSON

Washington Roebling hired a Brooklyn shipyard to build the caissons. The shipyard was a wise choice. First, it was nearby. Transporting the huge caissons to the tower sites would not be a big problem. Second, the caissons were basically upside-down boat hulls. It made sense for a shipbuilder to make them. Meanwhile, workers began to prepare the site of the Brooklyn-side tower. Using large steam-powered scoops and explosives, they removed as much sand, rock, and debris as possible from the tower site. In March 1870, a barge carried the first caisson from the shipyard to the Brooklyn tower site near the Fulton Ferry Landing. It measured 168 feet (51 m), and it was 14.5 feet (4.4 m) tall. The caisson was pushed off of the barge and kept afloat until workers began to sink it by building the stone tower structure on top of it.

Once the caisson struck bottom, pumps removed the water trapped inside the chamber. Workers then climbed down an air-shaft. They worked hard, digging up sand, rocks, and boulders with picks, hydraulic (water-powered) jacks, and steel stone breakers. Day after day, they dumped wheelbarrow load after wheelbarrow load of this debris into a shallow pool of water inside the caisson. Other workers used a large bucket, called a clam-digger, to scoop up the debris. The clam-digger was then sent up a water shaft to the top of the caisson. Workers on top of the caisson unloaded the debris and sent the clam-digger back down the shaft. At the beginning, clearing the debris took much longer than Roebling had planned—the caisson was sinking only 6 inches (15 cm) a day. He had to come up with a quicker way to make it to bedrock. After conducting some safety tests in the caisson, he had his workers use explosives to break up the large boulders.

DANGERS INSIDE THE CAISSON

The caisson gave workers space to dig down to the bedrock on the Brooklyn side. Conditions inside the underwater chamber, however, were dreadful—it was like being in a dark, soggy cave. Candles and lanterns made it very hot inside the caisson, and it was difficult to breathe. The compressed air pumped into the caisson made everyone's voice sound high-pitched. The depth under the water caused the workers' pulse (heart rate) to increase and created great pressure on their eardrums. Working in the caisson was dangerous, as well; the threat of a fire or a serious water leak was always present.

Washington Roebling lived in a house in Brooklyn Heights with his wife, Emily, and their son, John. He spent many hours inside the caisson, working alongside his men. He constantly worried about the conditions inside the chamber. The use of compressed air, burning candles, and explosives created a high fire risk. On December 2, 1870, a fire started. Because of the highly compressed air, the fire's flames could barely be seen, and there was very little smoke. Roebling stayed in the caisson all night trying to put it out. By morning, it appeared that the fire had been extinguished, but workers soon spotted smoke again. To make sure that the fire was completely extinguished, Roebling ordered his men out of the caisson. He had the compressed air turned off and the caisson flooded with water. The water was pumped out, and the air compressor pumped air back into the chamber.

Blowouts were another danger in the caisson. Sometimes the rising tide or a large ship passing the tower site would cause the caisson to shift slightly, and large bubbles of compressed air would escape from the bottom edge of the caisson. Each air

THE CAISSONS

Washington Roebling designed the caissons for the Brooklyn Bridge. These were complex devices: Each caisson had several holes in the roof that provided access to the hollow chamber inside. There were two shafts for workers, two shafts for transferring tools and supplies, and two water shafts for removing debris. Additional shafts held pipes for gas, air, and water. Men climbed through an air lock in the roof to get into and out of the caisson. Compressed air had to be pumped into the caisson constantly so the workers could breathe. The high air pressure inside the chamber also helped prevent the caisson's walls from collapsing because of the weight of the water around it and the stones on top of it.

bubble would soar to the surface, making a roaring sound as it reached the top. The blowouts spewed water, sand, and even fish into the air above the river. One of the biggest blowouts sent stones and other debris about 500 feet (152 m) high. From the shore, these looked like giant waterspouts. The blowouts scared the workmen, but they never caused much damage.

Meanwhile, stonemasons on top of the caisson set huge limestone blocks in place on the caisson's roof. As stone was added to the top, the caisson slowly sank closer to the solid bedrock each day. Each layer also built the tower up. Slowly, the Brooklyn tower began to take shape.

A MYSTERIOUS DISEASE

The caisson went deeper and deeper, and some workmen began to feel sick when they exited the chamber. They complained about pains in their arms and legs, dizziness, and vomiting. Similar symptoms had been reported at a bridge-building site in St. Louis. Bridge builder James Eads was using caissons to build foundations for a bridge that would cross the Mississippi River. Several of his workers complained that they had trouble breathing after working in a caisson; one man had even died soon after coming to the surface. Roebling had heard about this death and kept a close eye on his workers.

The illness suffered by caisson workers became known as caisson disease, which more and more workers in the Brooklyn caisson began to experience. Most of their symptoms were mild. Roebling spent as much time in the caisson as most of his workers. He, too, began to feel the unpleasant effects of caisson disease. His doctor ordered him to stay in bed to recover.

Although Roebling suffered from caisson disease, he remained in charge of building the bridge. To communicate with his engineering staff, he began dictating letters to Emily. She would write down his detailed instructions and then carry the letters to the other engineers. In doing so, she soon learned a lot about engineering. She became her husband's eyes and ears.

CAISSON DISEASE

Caisson disease occurs when nitrogen bubbles form in human tissue and blood as a person moves from highly pressurized air to normal air. It is also known as decompression sickness or the bends.

Body tissues contain small amounts of the common gases found in air—oxygen, carbon dioxide, and nitrogen. The tissues store larger amounts of these gases underwater because of the increase in air pressure. When an underwater worker or a diver comes up to the water's surface from a great depth, the air pressure drops dramatically. The excess gases, however, remain in the tissues. Neither extra oxygen nor extra carbon dioxide causes problems. These two gases are easily absorbed by the cells in the body or exhaled through the lungs. Excess nitrogen, however, can be problematic.

When the air pressure decreases too quickly, tiny nitrogen bubbles form in a person's body tissue and blood. These bubbles can cause breathing difficulty, coughing, chest pains, joint pains, and dizziness. In the worst cases, nitrogen bubbles can cause unconsciousness, blindness, and even paralysis or death. These symptoms can be avoided by having the person move, very slowly, from highly compressed air to normal air. This prevents the dangerous nitrogen bubbles from forming.

Emily checked on the progress of the bridge and reported back to Washington. At first, the other engineers and employees were taken aback that a woman was involved in the project. But Emily was smart, tactful, and friendly. Everyone who was connected with the bridge soon accepted her new role. Some bridge company officials, however, wanted the ailing Roebling removed from the project.

Work on the Brooklyn caisson was finally finished in March 1871. It rested on bedrock nearly 45 feet (13.7 m) below the East River. Workers carefully filled the inside chamber with concrete. The caisson would provide a solid foundation for the Brooklyn tower.

THE NEW YORK CAISSON

All of the hard work involved in sinking the caisson for the Brooklyn tower taught Roebling many valuable lessons. He used these lessons to make the work on the New York caisson safer. The river floor on the New York side, however, was much sandier than on the Brooklyn side. Roebling also faced a bigger problem: The bedrock on the New York side was much deeper. He would have to sink the caisson for the New York tower much lower—nearly twice as far.

The New York caisson was launched from a pier on East 6th Street in May 1871. By November, workers had sunk it to the riverbed at the tower site. As the digging inside the caisson progressed, it eventually passed the depth of the Brooklyn caisson. As it sank

Roebling worked underground so often that he contracted caisson disease, making him unable to supervise the aboveground construction of the towers. *Above*, workers wait while a supervisor examines their work on the Brooklyn tower in September 1872.

deeper and deeper, more and more workers began to suffer from caisson disease. Their symptoms became much worse than those experienced in the Brooklyn caisson. Soon after the New York caisson went below 60 feet (18.3 m), two workers died from the disease. Roebling, only somewhat recovered from his earlier case of the disease, went down in the New York caisson many times. He grew increasingly sicker and endured intense pains in his legs and arms, and began to faint when he returned to the surface. He hired a doctor to treat him and his workers. At that time, no one understood the cause of the disease or knew that rising to the surface slowly would prevent the symptoms. The doctor could only treat the workers' symptoms as best he could.

Roebling again was confined to his house as he suffered from caisson disease. Every day he wrote letters to the engineers for

BUILDING AMERICA NOW

WOODROW WILSON BRIDGE PROJECT

The Woodrow Wilson Bridge Project involved the construction of two side-by-side bascule drawbridges that span the Potomac River between Alexandria, Virginia, and Oxon Hill, Maryland. A bascule (French for "seesaw") bridge is a type of drawbridge that uses a counterweight to raise the bridge deck. When the counterweight is lowered, the hinged bridge deck swings up.

The first bridge opened in 2006, and the second bridge opened in 2008. They replaced the original Woodrow Wilson Bridge, built in 1961. (The original bridge was demolished in 2006 to make room for the second new bridge.) Population growth in the Maryland and Virginia suburbs of Washington, D.C., created more demand for crossing the Potomac River than the 6 lanes of the old bridge could handle. The new bridges have a total of 12 lanes and carry Interstate 95 and Interstate

Emily to deliver. He also worked long hours to finalize the design for the bridge's anchorages, the locations where the bridge's suspension cables would be secured in the ground.

In May 1872, the New York caisson had sunk 78.5 feet (23.9 m) deep. Roebling sent an order to his workers to stop digging. The caisson was still about 30 feet (9 m) short of the bedrock layer and appeared to be sitting on firmly compacted sand. There had been no sign of the sand layer shifting. Roebling weighed the risks involved and decided that the caisson was deep enough to provide a good foundation for the New York tower; he had the caisson chamber filled with concrete. He was taking a huge risk. It was possible that the enormous weight of the finished bridge could cause the tower to sink, shift, or even collapse. On the other hand, digging deeper would cost more lives and injury from caisson disease.

495 across the river. They are among the few drawbridges on the roadways of the Interstate Highway System. To reduce traffic stoppages, the new bridges are 20 feet (6 m) higher than the old bridge. They provide enough clearance for most boats; the drawbridges are used only when tall ships need to pass.

The bridges provide a good example of the use of concrete and steel in modern bridges. Workers erected concrete piers on the bridges' concrete-and-steel foundations. Next, they placed steel beams on top of the piers. Concrete was then poured to form the bridge deck.

The International Road Federation awarded the Woodrow Wilson Bridge Project its prestigious Global Road Achievement Award in 2007. The project won the award for keeping the large, $2.4 billion enterprise on schedule and within budget while protecting the environment and attending to the concerns of local communities.

A PUBLIC SCANDAL

In the era of the Brooklyn Bridge's construction, no major building project in New York could be built without being controlled by a New York politician named William "Boss" Tweed. The head of the city's Democratic Party, Tweed and his corrupt friends swindled millions of dollars out of New York City's treasury. They worked with contractors to overcharge the city for paving streets, installing sewers, and other public works. Authorities arrested Tweed in 1871. At his trial, Tweed confessed that New York Bridge Company president Henry Murphy had given him $60,000 to influence the New York City government to buy stock from the private bridge company. New York City's purchase of bridge stock was key to the bridge being built. Tweed also became a major stockholder in the bridge company and joined its board of directors.

After the Tweed bribe had been exposed, the New York state legislature passed a law that made the bridge public property. The bridge company's stockholders were paid off, and the bridge became a public roadway. This legislation also gave the bridge an official name: the New York and Brooklyn Bridge. The mayors and financial officers of New York and Brooklyn now had control of the bridge. Brooklyn would cover two-thirds of construction costs, and New York would pay for the rest. The management of the bridge did not change, however. Henry Murphy was selected as president of the new board of trustees, and William Kingsley took a seat on the bridge's executive committee. The scandal had made the bridge look bad in the eyes of the public. People began to wonder whether more corruption was going on behind the scenes.

THE TOWERS GO UP

The work underwater had been difficult and dangerous. It had taken workers two years to build the solid foundations for the towers. While the caissons were being situated, onlookers could

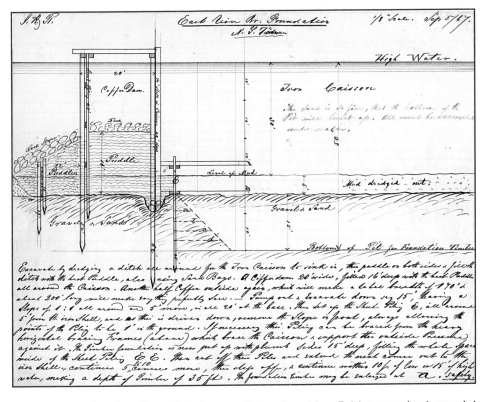

The caisson for the New York tower of the Brooklyn Bridge required special planning and design due to the depth of the bedrock on the New York side of the river. Excavation inside the caisson soon became too dangerous for the workers, as caisson disease incapacitated many of Roebling's employees and even killed some of them. *Above,* pages from Roebling's field notebooks detailing the plans for sinking and excavating the New York caisson.

see a great deal of activity on the water but no noticeable progress on the bridge. Some people began to speculate that the bridge would never be built. Construction on the Brooklyn tower soon provided evidence of progress.

To build the towers, workers used steam-hoisting machines—designed by Washington Roebling—that lifted huge granite stones into place. In November 1782, Roebling stopped work on

1872

PROGRESS UNSEEN

In his annual report to the bridge company in June 1872, Washington Roebling commented on the much-discussed lack of progress on the New York tower:

> To such of the general public as might imagine that no work had been done on the New York Tower, because they see no evidence of it above water. I should simply remark that the amount of the masonry and concrete laid on that foundation during the past winter, under water, is equal in quantity to the entire masonry of the Brooklyn tower visible today above the water line.

the tower; the winter weather made construction too difficult and dangerous. The Brooklyn tower now stood about 145 feet (44 m) above the water. Work on its large archway had begun.

Although Washington Roebling still suffered from the effects of caisson disease, he and Emily traveled to Germany that winter. The hot spring treatments at Wiesbaden had been suggested as a possible cure for his symptoms. The cure didn't work, and the Roeblings returned to Brooklyn in late 1873. Work on the towers was again suspended for winter. In early 1874, the Roeblings moved to Trenton, New Jersey, on doctor's orders, and stayed for three years. Despite his not being at the construction site, Roebling continued to direct the work. His plans were spelled out in such great detail that the assistant engineers had no trouble directing the construction of the towers.

COMPLETION OF THE TOWERS

While one bridge crew built the towers, another crew installed the bridge's anchorages. Anchorages are important parts of a suspension bridge because the bridge's main cables are secured to them. The cables transfer weight to them, so anchorages actually hold up much of a bridge's weight. Anchorages are usually embedded in large concrete blocks or even solid stone. Assistant engineer George McNulty supervised the installation of the anchorages in Brooklyn and New York.

Work on the Brooklyn anchorage began in February 1873. All of the various machines needed to make the bridge's cables were built on the Brooklyn anchorage. The Brooklyn tower was completed in June 1875 and stood 276.5 feet (84.3 m) above the average water level. (The water level under the bridges changes with the tides.) The Brooklyn anchorage was finished in November 1875; meanwhile, work on the New York anchorage had begun in May

When the towers were completed in 1875, workers began to build the anchorages of the bridge. Located at each of the towers, anchorages are large stone structures that hold the bridge's cables in place. Without them, the suspension cables would be unstable. Taken from atop the Brooklyn anchorage, this image shows men walking across a footbridge constructed for workers to get from one side of the river to the other.

1875. After another break for winter, work on the New York tower resumed in the spring of 1876 and was completed in July 1876. It was the same size as the Brooklyn tower. On July 11, the *Brooklyn Eagle* reported: "Before winter shall drive the workmen from their positions, we shall see the first strands of the great cable stretching aloft, spanning the river." A few weeks later, workers put the finishing touches on the New York anchorage.

The two towers standing in the East River provided a symbol of the growth of the United States. Seven years earlier, the Central Pacific and Union Pacific railroads had joined, creating the nation's first transcontinental railway. In March 1876, Alexander Graham Bell had invented the telephone. Just a few weeks earlier, Americans had celebrated the nation's centennial, or one-hundredth anniversary, on July 4. In August, Colorado would join the United States as the thirty-eighth state.

Construction on the Brooklyn Bridge had reached the halfway point. The towers were up and the anchorages were in place. The final two steps would be to make the cables and build the bridge's deck.

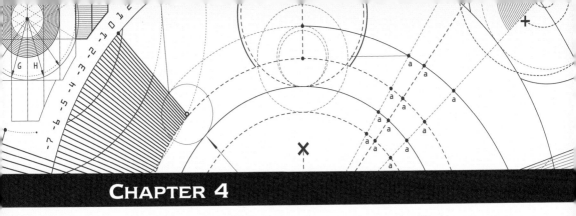

CHAPTER 4

The Cables and Deck

Although the Brooklyn and New York towers were completed, much more work had to be done. Washington Roebling turned his attention to the next step—installing the massive system of suspension cables that would hold up the bridge's deck. He had supervised the spinning cables on his father's Cincinnati bridge. He felt more at ease with this stage of the construction because he had more experience with cables.

INSTALLING THE CABLES

John Roebling's design for the Brooklyn Bridge called for four main cables. Each cable would contain about 3,500 miles (5,633 km) of steel wire. If made into a single strand, the wire in all four cables would stretch more than 14,000 miles (32,500 km)—about three-and-a-half times the distance from New York to Los Angeles. An amazing 6.8 million pounds (2,548 metric tons) of steel wire were needed to make the cables. The steel wire cables would be twice the strength of the iron wire cables John Roebling had used for his Niagara and Cincinnati bridges and would hold a load of 18,700 tons (16,965 metric tons).

To make sure that rain and the salty air that often hovered over the East River did not rust the cables, the wires would be galvanized. Galvanization is the process in which steel (or iron) is coated with the metal zinc. Zinc helps protect steel from the elements. John Roebling introduced an innovation: Galvanized steel had never before been used in a bridge. The traditional method of protecting the wire cables was to slather them with oil or grease or to paint them.

Each of the Brooklyn Bridge's cables would consist of 5,282 steel wires. Each of these wires would be a mere one-eighth-inch

HOW SUSPENSION BRIDGES WORK

Suspension bridges have four main parts: towers, cables, anchorages, and deck. The towers and cables hold up the deck. The anchorages secure the cables to the ground. The towers are built on foundations in the water. On top of the towers, devices called saddles carry the cables across the towers. Vertical cables, called suspenders, hang from the main cables. The bridge's deck, or roadway, is attached to the suspenders. Wires known as diagonal stays connect the towers to the deck.

John Roebling once said that a suspension bridge is a balance of opposites. The heavy deck pulls down on the main cables. The cables, anchored to each shore and weighed down by the deck, are always in tension (stretched tightly). The towers, which hold the weight of the cables and the deck, are always under compression (pushed down). One way to understand how a suspension bridge works is to imagine a clothesline. The clotheslines (the cables) run between two poles (the towers) and hold up drying clothes (the deck). Now imagine that the clotheslines continue past the T-shaped poles, run down to the ground, and are staked into the ground. The weight of the clothes pulls down on the clothesline, stretching it tightly and pulling down on the poles.

(3 mm) thick. Workers put together 278 wires to form a single strand. Next, they bound 19 strands together to form a bundle. Each bundle would be wrapped with a protective layer of soft iron wire. The finished cables would be 15.5 inches (39 cm) in diameter.

THE TRAVELER

Suspension bridge cables are too long and heavy to be made in a factory and then installed on the bridge's towers. Instead, workers make the cables on top of the bridge. They stretch the wires one at a time: from one anchorage, up and over the towers, to the other anchorage.

Work on the Brooklyn Bridge's cables began in the summer of 1876. Workers loaded a large reel onto a barge docked at a pier on the Brooklyn shore. The reel held more than 3,000 feet (914 m) of heavy steel rope. Workers would use this rope—called the "traveler" or "working rope"—to haul the hundreds of cable wires back and forth across the towers.

On the morning of August 11, sailors tied the barge to their tugboat to take it across the river. They could not cross until the tide was calm and the busy river had no ship traffic. Their chance came at around 9:00 A.M. The tugboat set off and, in less than 10 minutes, pulled the barge across the river. As the barge moved along, workers unwound the wire behind the boat. Workers on both towers then used hemp ropes attached to steam engines to hoist the rope to the top of each tower. The middle part of the rope remained underwater.

The engineers had to wait until there were no ships between the towers before they could raise the rope. They waited about two hours. At approximately 11:30 A.M., master mechanic E.F. Farrington gave a signal, and workers turned on a steam engine that tightened the rope. It took only a few minutes for the last part of the rope to pop out of the water. Spectators on land and aboard boats cheered loudly. In a few minutes, the rope was in position, about 200 feet (61 m) above the river.

Back on the Brooklyn shore, the tugboat started back with another barge, carrying a second reel of heavy steel rope. By 3:30 P.M., workers had hoisted the second rope into position. Other workers spliced, or joined together, the two ends of the rope at the New York anchorage. The traveler was now one long loop. It stretched from the Brooklyn anchorage, over the two towers, to the New York anchorage, and back again. Measuring nearly 6,800 feet (2,072 m), it was more than a mile (2 km) long.

Washington Roebling had returned to Brooklyn for the making of the bridge's cables. He still suffered severely from caisson disease, however, and was too ill to make it to the bridge site to see the traveler installed. He could not leave his house. Shortly after noon, he received a telegraph: THE FIRST WIRE ROPE REACHED ITS POSITION AT ELEVEN AND ONE HALF O'CLOCK. WAS RAISED IN SIX MINUTES. Another telegraph arrived later that afternoon, informing him that the traveler was in position.

A *New York Herald* editorial proclaimed that the traveler was "the engagement ring in the marriage preparation of the two cities." In New York and Brooklyn, the bridge became a hot topic of conversation. The thin rope connecting the two cities helped boost enthusiasm for the much-maligned bridge.

THE FIRST CROSSING

Newspapers reported that the next step would be to send a man across the rope. More than 100 people, the youngest of whom was 12 years old, showed up at the bridge office to volunteer. To quiet the crowd, assistant engineer C.C. Martin told everyone that a bridge employee would be the first person to make the river crossing. The engineers chose E.F. Farrington, who was nearly 60 years old. Some observers ridiculed the decision because of his age. Farrington, however, was in great physical shape. He was also considered the best bridge mechanic in the country and had many years of experience working with wire rope.

The crossing was scheduled for the morning of August 25, 1877. Farrington arrived at the Brooklyn Bridge office wearing a new suit and a new straw hat. He was ready for his big day.

Mechanic E.F. Farrington, one of the country's best bridge workers, was chosen to be the first to cross the East River via the Brooklyn Bridge. Sitting on a small wooden seat held up by rope, Farrington waved his straw hat at 10,000 cheering people as he flew over the river *(above)*.

Spectators jammed both shorelines. Boat captains anchored their vessels at the best viewing spots in the East River. In the next day's newspapers, reporters would estimate that 10,000 people had gathered to watch the momentous event.

Workers made final adjustments to a system of belts and pulleys. By 11:00 A.M., they turned on the steam engines. The traveler began to move across the towers. The workers spent about 30 minutes sending it back and forth, to make sure that there were no kinks in it. After a break for lunch, Farrington climbed onto a boatswain's chair. The swinglike contraption consisted of a board seat with four ropes attached to each corner. Workers attached the boatswain's chair to the traveler at the Brooklyn anchorage. The heavy steel rope was nearly an inch (2.5 cm) thick and could hold more than 1,000 pounds (450 kg). To many observers, it appeared much too flimsy to ride on.

At 1:30 P.M., workers started the engine again. The traveler starting moving. Aboard the boatswain's chair, Farrington started to ride toward the Brooklyn tower. The spectators cheered wildly. It took nearly four minutes for Farrington to travel from the anchorage to the tower. One he reached the tower, he carefully climbed out of the boatswain's chair.

Farrington quickly moved to the other side of the tower and climbed back into the boatswain's chair. He took a deep breath as he prepared for the long ride across the East River. The engine started again, and the master mechanic shot out across the river. From a distance, the traveler was not visible. All that most spectators could see was a person flying though the air. For his part, Farrington was having a grand time. He waved his hat excitedly as he glided toward the New York tower.

It took less than seven minutes for Farrington to reach the New York tower. A few minutes later, he embarked on the last leg of the journey, from the New York tower to the New York anchorage. As he reached the shore, church bells peeled, factory whistles shrieked, and boat horns blared. The *New York Times* described the scene as "a perfect pandemonium."

BUILDING AMERICA NOW

OHIO RIVER BRIDGES PROJECT

The state of Kentucky is building two bridges as part of a project to improve transportation in the Louisville area. Since the era of the Brooklyn Bridge, population increases and the introduction of motor vehicles have greatly multiplied the transportation needs of the United States. Bridge projects have become much more complicated. Bridges are now parts of complex regional transportation systems.

The Ohio River Bridges Project consists of three elements. Two new bridges will link Louisville with southern Indiana. (Two Louisville bridges already cross the Ohio River.) The busy interchange between three major interstate highways (I-71, I-64, and I-65) will be rebuilt to improve the flow of traffic.

In December 2006, state officials approved the design of a three-tower, cable-stayed bridge to be built in downtown Louisville. Cable-stayed bridges are similar to suspension bridges, but their cables are not anchored to the shore. Instead, the towers support the entire weight of cables, which are connected to the deck. State officials also approved the design for a bridge to be located eight miles east of Louisville. It will be a median-tower, cable-stayed, center-cable bridge. Both bridges will have protected lanes for pedestrians and bicyclists. They will also have shoulder lanes for vehicle breakdowns and emergency access. The bridge piers placed in the water will be round rather than square; this round shape will allow water to pass by more easily. The round piers will also collect less debris. State officials held public meetings to give residents the chance to take part in the bridge-design selection process.

Construction on these two new Ohio River bridges began in 2007, and officials estimate that the bridges will open in 2020. The cost of the two bridges and interchange renovation is estimated at $2.46 billion.

Farrington's journey had taken only 22 minutes. Crowds around the New York anchorage pressed forward to congratulate him. Bridge officials whisked him into the bridge office—they had to sneak him out a back door and onto a boat to Brooklyn to keep him from being mobbed by well-wishers. He told reporters that he was honored to receive so much attention. His main goal, however, had not been to entertain the crowds. He wanted to make sure his workers knew that he believed the traveler was safe. When the cable-making process began, they would be working on the traveler under much more dangerous conditions. In his book *Concise Description of the East River Bridge* (1881), Farrington later wrote, "The ride gave me a magnificent view, and such pleasing sensations as probably I shall never experience again."

After six years of setbacks, criticisms, and lack of public enthusiasm, Farrington's crossing changed the way people looked at the bridge. In the mind of the public, the Brooklyn Bridge changed from a vague, future possibility to a real structure that could be imagined.

SPINNING AND SPINNING

All the machinery for running the ropes and wires was located at the Brooklyn anchorage. Steam engines operated the system of wheels, pulleys, and belts. A series of cogwheels turned a 12-foot (3.7-m) wheel that moved the traveler back and forth across the river. Most of the workers had never worked on a bridge before. The engineers, along with Farrington and the other experienced bridge builders, had to teach them the proper way to spin the cables. It was a difficult and dangerous job: The workers had to make sure that each individual wire was in precisely the right position to form a uniform strand. In turn, each strand would have to be in exactly the right position to form a flawless bundle.

Before work on the cables began, a series of wire ropes was spliced to the traveler and sent back and forth over the towers.

These ropes would be used to hold up platforms, which workers would stand on to bind the wires for the cables. Then, more wire ropes were strung across the river. These ropes would support a footbridge, which the workers would use to carry tools and supplies to the work sites. To prevent wind from blowing it away, workers attached two cables from the towers to the bottom of the footbridge.

The 4-foot-wide (1.2-m) wood-plank footbridge was finished in February 1877. Wire handrails were strung on each side. The footbridge stood about 180 feet (55 m) above the water, approximately 60 feet (18 m) higher than the bridge's roadway would eventually sit. The footbridge now connected the two cities. Several newspaper reporters made the risky trip across the footbridge's narrow wooden slats. One reporter wrote that his trip across the footbridge "produced sensations in . . . [my] head— and stomach—never experienced before." Another reporter, like many others, had lost his nerve and had not been able to make it across. He wrote his article anyway.

On May 29, 1877, the engineers tested the cable-spinning system to make sure that everything was working correctly. A large reel of slender steel wire was positioned at the Brooklyn anchorage. Workers attached the steel wire to a big iron wheel, called the "carrier." They attached the carrier to the traveler rope and turned on a steam engine. The engine tugged on the traveler, which began to move. The traveler took the carrier and the wire attached to it up and over the Brooklyn tower, across the river, over the New York tower, and down to the New York anchorage. The engine was stopped. Workers at each anchorage cut the wire and spliced it to their anchorage. Another wire was attached to the traveler on the New York side, and the engine pulled it back across the towers. The test went well. Washington Roebling had estimated that the cable-spinning equipment could go through about 40 miles (64 km) of wire a day. Crews began to make many reels of wire for the cable; each stored 10 miles (16 km) of wire.

As bridge construction continued, the dangerous nature of the work became apparent to the public whenever there was a fatal accident at the site. In spite of the potential hazards, men continued to seek employment at the bridge. *Above*, men audition for the job of bridge painter by walking up and down the main cables.

On June 11, workers began to make the four main cables. The two downriver cables were made first. The machinery was set up in a way that two cables could be built up at the same time. Although the traveler was a complete loop, workers did not send it around in a circle. Instead, they sent it back and forth in a semicircle. The wires were gathered parallel to each other—imagine holding a handful of long spaghetti strands together. Although a single strand was not very strong, many strands held together would be strong enough to hold up a heavy bridge.

Two carriers moved across the traveler and carried the wire back and forth across the river. As the traveler pulled one wire carrier from Brooklyn to New York, it pulled another one from New York to Brooklyn. Workers stationed along the traveler made sure that the wire remained tight. When the carriers reached each anchorage, the traveler would stop. Workers on each end cut the wires and attached them to their anchorage. They attached two more wires and sent the traveler across the river in the opposite direction. The carriers keep going back and forth until 278 wires (the amount needed to make a strand) were strung. Workers rode down the strand in buggies (similar to small ski lifts) and tied the wires together every 15 feet (5 m).

Washington Roebling had calculated that it would take 18 months to finish the cables. Despite weather delays, breaks in the wires, and other problems, the cable spinning went faster than expected. The cable-making equipment was able to go through 50 miles (80 km) of wire a day. Soon, all four cables were under construction. Four carriers were shuttling across the river.

One newspaper announced, "The network of wires across the East River is rapidly beginning to look something like a bridge." Another newspaper commented on the progress:

> There is something colossal in the look of the East River piers as
> they show in the morning sunlight; the ropes already connecting

the two piers seem like slender threads, and as the vessels pass and repass under them some idea may be formed of what may be the effect when the graceful upper wire structure is completed, with the roadway crowded with passengers and vehicles of all descriptions and the high-masted clipper and coasting traders passing underneath.

Washington Roebling also followed the progress of his workers making the cables. He used binoculars to watch from the window of his house.

Meanwhile, the footbridge became a major attraction. People from all walks of life applied for permission to cross it. The bridge company allowed many of them to do so, but they turned down a woman who wanted to ride a horse across the bridge. The bridge company's president, Henry Murphy, said: "We don't want to turn the bridge into a show." Many who received permission took several steps and then crawled back on their hands and knees. A few froze midway. Workers had to help them back to solid ground.

A CONTROVERSY

On Thanksgiving Day, 1877, one of the wires snapped. The assistant engineers sent a piece of it to Roebling, who examined the wire. In a letter to assistant engineer William Paine, he wrote that it was "brittle as glass." He angrily told Paine that the wire was "worthless." The bridge company had awarded the contract to supply the wire for the cables to a Brooklyn businessman named J. Lloyd Haight. Upon investigation, the bridge company discovered that Haight had substituted poor-quality wire for the high-quality wire purchased by the bridge.

The wire contract had originally been awarded to John A. Roebling's Sons, who had submitted the lowest bid. Although Washington Roebling had sold his interest in the company, several bridge trustees worried that a conflict of interest remained;

the public might assume that Roebling's family was profiting too much from the contract. The bridge company had quietly transferred the wire-supply contract to the politically well-connected Haight instead.

Roebling now faced a big problem: No one knew how much bad wire had already been spun into the cables. It would be very expensive and time consuming to remove the partially finished cables and start over again. It was unlikely that the bridge company would agree to that solution. Roebling recalculated the wire strength and ordered his engineers to add 150 wires to each cable. His father had designed the cables to be six times stronger than necessary to hold the weight of the roadway. Roebling concluded that, by adding more wire to the weaker wire, the cables would still be four times as strong as necessary.

Roebling remained very sick from the effects of caisson disease. Emily spent most of her days writing down his detailed instructions and delivering them to the assistant engineers. She continued to meet with officials from the bridge company and to inspect the work on the bridge. The Roeblings had an unusual relationship for the era. Some people grumbled that a woman should not be given so much power for such an important project. Emily, however, silenced most doubters. Without her intelligence and hard work, the bridge company would likely have stopped the construction of the bridge or hired a new chief engineer.

THE WORK CONTINUES

Workers kept spinning cable. They wrapped more than 14,000 miles (22,530 km) of steel wire together to form the bridge's four main cables. Another group of workers strung suspender cables downward from the top of the main cables. The suspender cables would be attached to the roadway's steel floor beams. They would support the bridge's road and walkway. Other workers installed special steel wires called diagonal stays. The suspenders and

The deck of the Brooklyn Bridge was originally slated to be constructed of iron trusses. In the years it had taken for the project to come together, the development of a lightweight steel that was just as strong as iron prompted a design change from Washington Roebling.

stays would give the Brooklyn Bridge its famous weblike appearance. Unlike the main cables, the suspenders and stays would be woven like rope.

One of the worst accidents during the construction of the bridge occurred on June 14, 1878. A cable strand broke loose from the New York anchorage, whipped over the New York tower, and plunged into the East River. The loose wire killed two workers and injured several others. The tragedy made the dangers of the bridge more obvious to the public. The bridge company did not keep records of deaths on the bridge. Washington Roebling later noted that 20 workers died, plus his father. Others estimated the number to be higher.

BUILDING THE DECK

On October 5, 1878, workers finished making the four main cables. The only remaining step was to build the deck. All the other parts of the bridge had been built to hold it up. The deck had to be strong enough to support all of the bridge's traffic: commuter trains, carriages, wagons, and pedestrians. John Roebling designed the deck to be made out of panels of iron framework known as *trusses*. The trusses were heavy and stiff, which would prevent wind from making the bridge sway. High winds had caused many suspension bridges to collapse.

The suspenders strung down from the cables would hold the deck, which would be installed panel by panel. Each panel would be a 12-foot (3.6-m) section of steel trusses. Washington decided to have the trusses made out of steel instead of iron, as his father had specified. Because of advances in the manufacturing of steel, the lighter-weight steel trusses would have the same strength as iron trusses. Workers began to install the truss

LOOKING AHEAD

The thousands who daily cross the ferries and look up to the lofty towers that rise on either hand above the water, and note the strands that stretch across the intervening space, hardly recognize that the cable making of the great structure is nearing its completion. . . . [B]y the time the cold weather sets in we shall see the four great cables completed and ready for the . . . roadway of the bridge. It has been steady and patient work—wire upon wire and strand upon strand—through heat and cold and storm and calm, and now this branch of the great enterprise nears its end, and another department of the work of construction appears in the near future.

—*Brooklyn Eagle* editorial, August 8, 1878

panels, beginning at the towers and working outward. The two ends of the deck advanced over the East River and slowly moved toward each other.

Delays in steel shipments slowed the work on the deck. Workers finally finished its understructure in December 1881. While the deck was being finished, crews built roads on each side of the river leading to the bridge. Construction began on the train stations to be located at each end of the bridge, as well as on the bridge's pedestrian promenade. The promenade would be built 18 feet (5.5 m) above the roadway for carriages and wagons. By April 1883, all of the trusswork on the bridge was finished, and only a few minor tasks remained. After 14 years of setbacks, physical suffering, and mental anguish, Washington Roebling informed the bridge trustees that the Brooklyn Bridge was ready to open to the public.

CHAPTER 5

The Bridge Opens

By the spring of 1883, the bridge was ready for pedestrians and traffic. During the 14 years that the bridge had been under construction, Brooklyn's population increased by 180,000, and New York's grew by more than 200,000. The telephone had been invented. The nation's first electric lighting system had been installed in New York City. Building the bridge had taken nearly three times longer than John Roebling's estimate of five years. Construction costs topped $15 million, tripling Roebling's estimate of $5 million.

PREPARATIONS

The bridge company decided to open the bridge to the public on May 24, 1883. Workers still needed to install electric lights and railings for the pedestrian walkway. The train terminals on each end of the bridge remained under construction—they would not open until autumn. For the first few months, only pedestrians, livestock, and carriages and wagons would cross the bridge.

Workers removed the wood scaffolding from the towers. Everyone could now see what the bridge really looked like. John Roebling's vision had finally been realized. The finished roadway curved up to the gothic towers and over the river. The bridge's hundreds of suspenders and diagonal stays made it look like a spiderweb from a distance. For the people of Brooklyn, it would provide easy, year-round access to New York City. For New Yorkers, it would provide a place to escape the crowded city streets. For everyone, it would be something to behold. The editors of *Scientific American* wrote:

> The bridge is a marvel of beauty viewed from the level of the river. In looking at its vast stretch, not only over the river between the towers, but over the inhabited, busy city shore, it appears to have a character of its own far above the drudgeries and exactions of the lower business levels.

Not everyone shared this rosy view of the bridge. Those who remembered the political scandals that involved Boss Tweed saw it as a symbol of political corruption. Others would never forget that poor-quality steel had been spun into the main cables. Some bridge workers would live with the horrors of working in the caissons for the rest of their lives. The families of workers who died on the job would keep grieving.

Emily Roebling continued to serve as the go-between for her husband. Washington Roebling's health had improved a little, and his vision had cleared up. Although he could walk again, he remained weak and tired easily. Construction was winding down, but Emily went to the bridge almost every day.

Before the opening ceremonies, the engineers wanted to test the roadway. They planned to send a carriage over the bridge, to see how a horse's trot affected the structure's stability. Washington suggested that Emily be the person to ride in the carriage; the bridge trustees and engineers agreed. Emily Roebling would be the first person to cross the Brooklyn Bridge. One May morning,

Because Washington Roebling was debilitated by caisson disease, Emily Roebling (*above*) helped her husband with his work on the bridge. From delivering detailed instructions to the assistant engineers to inspecting work and construction sites, Emily became an important factor in the bridge's construction and completion.

Emily climbed aboard a carriage on the Brooklyn side. With a coachman at the reins, the carriage crossed the bridge. Along the way, workers stopped to cheer the crossing. They doffed their hat and caps to Mrs. Roebling.

Washington Roebling and several bridge officials suggested that the bridge open quietly, with little fanfare. Most bridge officials and Brooklyn politicians, however, insisted on a huge, official celebration. Roebling worried about crowd safety—a large celebration would attract many people to the bridge. He also was concerned that the ceremony's fireworks would be shot off too close to the bridge. The bridge trustees issued 7,000 tickets for entry onto the bridge on opening day and distributed 6,000 tickets for the official ceremony. It would be held in the Brooklyn-side train terminal.

The celebration of the bridge's opening would be the biggest bash in New York since the opening of the Erie Canal in 1825. There was no doubt that it would be the most spectacular event in Brooklyn's history. Brooklyn mayor Seth Low announced that the bridge's opening on May 25, 1883, would be called the "People's Day." He proclaimed the day an official holiday. Brooklyn schools would cancel classes so students could experience history. Low also encouraged stores and businesses to close.

The Roeblings decided that Washington could not attend the official ceremonies. Emily, however, wanted to make sure that her husband received the acclaim he deserved. To persuade dignitaries to visit Roebling, Emily planned to host a reception at their home. The Roeblings' reception would take place at 7:00 P.M., after the official ceremonies. Among the guests she invited were bridge officials, local politicians, New York's governor, and even the president of the United States.

On the evening of Saturday, May 19, some of the people of New York and Brooklyn received a surprise. Between 11:00 P.M. and midnight, workers tested the bridge's electric lighting system—they wanted to make sure the lights worked on opening day. The electricity was turned on, and the bridge's lights began to glow. Hundreds of lightbulbs lit up the bridge. The strings of light crossed the river, tracing a line between Brooklyn and New York.

OPENING DAY

On Friday, May 24, 1883, more than 100,000 visitors descended on New York to join in the celebration of the Brooklyn Bridge's opening. Hotels sold out. The entire city bristled with flags and red, white, and blue banners. Getting close to the bridge was nearly impossible; the streets around it were packed with people. Sellers worked the crowds. They offered all sorts of souvenirs, from buttons to models of the bridge. People filled the nearby piers, rooftops, and building windows. Ships of almost every imaginable type packed the river. Six U.S. Navy warships sat in the harbor and river. The Brooklyn ferries were still operating; many people rode back and forth, enjoying some of the best views of the bridge.

There was even a little danger in the air. Some members of the city's large Irish population had voiced their anger over the celebration. The ceremonies were being held on Queen Victoria's birthday, an important holiday in Ireland at the time. Baseless rumors of Irish thugs causing trouble—even blowing up the bridge—made their way around the city.

At first, the weather looked dismal. By midmorning, however, the threatening clouds had blown over. The sun shone brightly. Many viewed the sudden change in the weather as a benevolent sign from above.

As in New York, flags were flying and buildings were covered in bunting throughout Brooklyn. One department store window sign read: "Babylon had her hanging garden, Egypt her pyramid, Athens her Acropolis, Rome her Athenaeum; so Brooklyn has her Bridge." On the other side of the river, the New York Stock Exchange, schools, and some stores remained open, but they were nearly empty. The *New York Times* later expressed surprise at the enthusiastic reaction of New Yorkers. An editorial read,

"There could have been no special cause of congratulation, since not one in one thousand of them will be likely to have occasion to use the new structure except for curiosity." Workers removed the fence on the New York side. A line of policemen held back the surging mass of spectators.

The ceremonies in Brooklyn began promptly at 12:40 in the afternoon. Three regiments of soldiers marched toward the bridge. Mayor Seth Low led the more than 200 city officials, bridge trustees, and special guests who followed the soldiers. Among them was Emily Roebling, riding in her carriage. Crowds lined the route to the bridge. When the marchers reached the bridge, most of the dignitaries entered the train terminal, where the official ceremony would take place. Mayor Low, bridge trustee William Kingsley, and a few other dignitaries followed one regiment of soldiers onto the bridge.

The day's guest of honor, President Chester A. Arthur, would cross the bridge from New York. Dressed in a black coat, a white tie, and a fashionable black beaver hat, Arthur was cheered wildly as he traveled from his hotel to the bridge. Accompanied by New York governor Grover Cleveland, Arthur eventually made his way through the crowds. When he reached the bridge, the *New York Sun* later reported that he "looked with evident admiration at the structure."

Following a huge band, a regiment of marching soldiers, and New York mayor Franklin Edson, Arthur and Cleveland walked up the bridge's roadway. Kingsley met them at the New York tower and escorted them across the bridge. Seven thousand ticket holders crowded the roadways on each side of the promenade, straining to catch a glimpse of the president and the governor. When the procession reached the Brooklyn tower, Seth Low officially welcomed Arthur, Cleveland, and Edson to Brooklyn.

On cue, the navy warships began to fire blank rounds from their cannons. Steam whistles shrieked, and bells rang out. More cannons boomed, and thousands of people cheered wildly. An editorial in the next day's *New York Sun* observed, "The climax of fourteen years' suspense seems to have been reached, since the President of the United States of America had walked dry shod to Brooklyn from New York." The entourage walked to the train terminal for the official ceremonies. The people in the terminal gave Arthur a standing ovation as he entered.

The three-hour program featured many different speakers. The president of the bridge trustees, James Stranahan, presided over the ceremonies. Each of the ceremony's many speakers seemed to have a different idea about what the bridge meant. In *The Great Bridge* (2001), David McCullough records the remarks of the speakers: One called it "an astounding exhibition of the power of man to change the face of nature." Another called it "a wonder of Science." Still another referred to the bridge as a monument to "enterprise, skill, faith, and endurance." All of the speakers reached a similar conclusion, however—they agreed that the bridge represented a victory for the human will and stood as a symbol of the nation's progress.

The major speakers represented the bridge trustees, the city of Brooklyn, and the city of New York. On behalf of the bridge trustees, William Kingsley presented the Brooklyn Bridge to the two cities. Mayor Low and the Reverend Richard Storrs spoke for Brooklyn. Mayor Edson and Congressman Abram Hewitt spoke for New York. In his speech, Seth Low may have best captured the spirit of the day:

> The beautiful and stately structure fulfills the fondest hope. . . . The impression upon the visitor is one of astonishment that grows with every visit. No one who has been upon it can ever forget it. . . . Not one shall see it and not feel prouder to be a man.

Hewitt compared John Roebling to Italian Renaissance artist and engineer Leonardo da Vinci. He praised Washington Roebling, telling the crowd that he was a better engineer than his father. He remarked that Emily Roebling would be "inseparably

Concerned over safety issues, Washington Roebling suggested a quieter opening ceremony for the Brooklyn Bridge, but city officials rejected the idea. They planned a large celebration, featuring U.S. Navy ships, fireworks, grand speeches, and several important dignitaries. President Chester A. Arthur *(above center)* attended the event and was one of the first people to walk across the bridge.

associated with all that is admirable in human nature, and with all that is wonderful in the constructive world of art." Hewitt also addressed the bridge's critics. He denied that there had been any fraud in the building of the bridge. According to Hewitt, Boss Tweed had stolen no money, and none of the bridge company's assets had been spent dishonestly. Hewitt finished by declaring that the Brooklyn Bridge was the finest creation of the century. From the perspective of Hewitt and other business leaders, labor and capital had successfully worked together. Using the century's newest technologies and know-how, they had built a monument to the nation's future. An editorial in the *Brooklyn Eagle* that morning offered a similar message: "This splendid structure thrown across the river . . . is not only a good in itself but a sure promise of the immeasurable greater good to come."

After the official ceremony, President Arthur, Governor Cleveland, and the other invited guests made their way to the reception at the Roeblings' Brooklyn Heights home. Eyewitnesses later recalled that Arthur sincerely praised the engineer as they shook hands. The president left after about an hour; he was due at a dinner hosted by Mayor Low down the block. (President Arthur would later end his busy day by attending a reception in his honor at the Brooklyn Academy of Music.) Roebling, exhausted from the day's events, went back upstairs. Many guests noted how slowly he climbed the stairs.

The bridge had opened up to the 7,000 ticket holders at 5:00 P.M. They walked around the bridge and looked closely at its details. They enjoyed its panoramic view of the harbor and the skylines of the two cities. When evening fell, the fireworks display began. Hundred of thousands watched as more than 14 tons (12.7 metric tons) of fireworks exploded over the harbor. More than 10,000 pieces were set off, and the fireworks lasted for about an hour. For the grand finale, 500 rockets were fired at once. As described in a newspaper the next day, they "broke into millions of stars and a shower of golden rain which descended upon the bridge and river."

THE GRAND DISPLAY OF FIREWORKS AND ILLUMINATIONS
AT THE OPENING OF THE GREAT SUSPENSION BRIDGE BETWEEN NEW YORK AND BROOKLYN
ON THE EVENING OF MAY 24th, 1883.

The highlight of the opening ceremony for the Brooklyn Bridge was its elaborate fireworks show at the end of the day. People who were lucky enough to get tickets stood on the bridge and watched as a thrilling display of fireworks lit up the harbor in a fitting introduction to the latest wonder of the world.

When the fireworks ended, both sides of the river exploded in noise. Bells rang, musicians played their instruments, steam whistles blew, and people yelled until they were hoarse. The next day's edition of the *New York Tribune* noted, "Hardly had the last falling spark died out, when the moon rose slowly from the further tower and sent a broad beam like a benediction across the river."

The day's final official event, the reception for the president at the Brooklyn Academy of Music, was a huge success. Eyewitnesses recounted that Arthur had a merry time. Officials in both cities later said that the "People's Day" festivities drew the largest crowd ever in New York. Many people would remember it as the biggest spectacle of their lives.

OPEN TO THE PUBLIC

The bridge trustees had announced that the bridge would open to the public at midnight. Huge crowds swarmed the entrances on both sides of the bridge. The police corralled people into holding pens as they waited for the bridge to open. Many waited for more than six hours. At the stroke of midnight, toll collectors on the Brooklyn side opened the windows of their tollbooths. People paid a one-cent toll and rushed onto the bridge. The tollbooths on the New York side opened 10 minutes later. On this side, the crowd became testy, and there was a sudden push toward the entrance. One observer noted that the crowd was "willing to throttle the police and pound one another to mince-meat." Police used their billy clubs to control the most unruly members of the crowd.

People poured across the bridge all night, and crowds were still streaming onto the bridge at daybreak. The first-day ticket holders had enjoyed the bridge at a leisurely pace. Over the next few days, the rest of the public had a much different experience. Pedestrians jammed the promenade at all hours of the day and night. On May 25, the first full day of operation, slightly more than 150,000 people crossed the bridge on foot. About 1,800 carriages, wagons, and other vehicles made the trip across the bridge. One policeman observed, "It seems to me as if the people have gotten the bridge craze."

Despite being hailed as the Eighth Wonder of the World, the Brooklyn Bridge had a troubling start. A sense of fear and physical danger hung over the bridge. Newspapers reported that some young men raced their horses across the bridge and recklessly knocked down pedestrians. The police received complaints about kids throwing rocks off of the bridge onto boats and rooftops. Pickpockets worked the crowds. One newspaper editorial clucked, "When you see a man with his coat turned off of him and a lady with her hat jammed over her eyes it is pretty safe to say that they have crossed the bridge. That noble structure has thus far been ruled by the mob."

On May 31, 1883, one of Washington Roebling's greatest fears came true. About 20,000 people had crowded onto the bridge. Because it was Memorial Day, no tolls were being charged. The

BUILDING AMERICA NOW

THE NEW BENICIA-MARTINEZ BRIDGE

The New Benicia-Martinez Bridge opened on August 25, 2007. It spans the Carquinez Strait, linking the northern California cities of Benicia and Martinez. The bridge carries northbound vehicles along busy Interstate 680. It is a concrete box-girder bridge, made with concrete segments. The bridge is 8,790 feet (2,679 m) long and 82 feet (25 m) wide, and it has five traffic lanes. It sits beside the original Benicia-Martinez Bridge (1962) and a railroad bridge.

The bridge builders used several innovation construction methods for this structure. They cast, or made, the bridge's 335 concrete segments in place (at their exact, final location). They used a specially made air-bubble curtain system to reduce the environmental impact of the installation of the bridge's piers. This curtain stopped the sound waves made by the machinery pounding the concrete piers into the ground underneath the water.

The new bridge was built to lessen traffic congestion, lower the number of traffic accidents, and improve the movement of freight. Its construction allowed lanes for pedestrians and bicycles to be added to the old bridge. It was built to support a proposed future commuter railway and cost $1.3 billion to build. (As a comparison, the 1962 Benicia-Martinez Bridge cost $25 million.)

crowds were enjoying the holiday and basking in the warm, sunny weather, when overcrowding on a stairway turned into a tragedy. A woman tripped and fell while trying to walk down the stairs from the promenade. The people behind her could not stop—the crowds behind them pushed them forward. More people fell down the stairs, and bodies began to pile on top of each other. Panic spread through the crowd as people tried to flee. Because of the crush of bodies, some people in the crowd had blood oozing out of their ears and noses. Coins, shoes, and other items fell onto the rooftops beneath the bridge. In all, 12 people were trampled to death.

After the Memorial Day tragedy, pedestrian traffic dropped. The bridge craze seemed to have ended. By September, however, the crowds had returned to the bridge. The trains began to run on September 24. Within a year, 37,000 people were crossing the bridge every day. In their first year of service, the trains carried more than 9 million passengers. By 1885, the trains ran 24 hours a day and carried nearly 20 million passengers.

The ornate train stations featured fancy ironwork, stone pillars, and large plate-glass windows. Steam engines moved a steel cable, which pulled the dark-red train cars back and forth across the bridge. Commuters paid 5 cents each way. To cross the roadway, a horse rider paid 5 cents. The toll for a horse-drawn carriage or wagon was 10 cents. For those who herded livestock over the bridge, cows cost 5 cents each and sheep and hogs 2 cents each. Pedestrians paid a 3-cent toll to cross the bridge. Several state legislators had already proposed making the crossing free for pedestrians.

Operating the bridge required a large workforce. Washington Roebling had resigned as chief engineer on July 9, 1883. The bridge trustees promoted C.C. Martin, his chief assistant, to succeed him. Martin employed more than 200 full-time employees, including assistant engineers; blacksmiths, carpenters, painters, and oilers; train engineers, conductors, and dispatchers; toll collectors; and policemen and firemen. Martin would serve as the bridge's chief engineer until 1902.

A PART OF THE CITY

For New York and Brooklyn residents, the bridge fulfilled its basic functions: It stimulated growth in both cities. It put Brooklyn on the map. It provided safe, reliable, year-round transportation across the East River. It provided New Yorkers relief from the city. Anyone could walk out onto its elevated promenade and view the harbor and the skylines. (Even today, none of the world's large bridges have an elevated pedestrian walkway.) It became one of the most soul-stirring spots in the United States. Hundreds of thousands of tourists visited it—the bridge was among the first things immigrants saw at they entered New York Harbor. Many immigrants took particular pride in the bridge: A German immigrant designed the bridge, and many immigrant workers had built it.

Soon, the Brooklyn Bridge became notorious for two things: people jumping off of it and stories about hucksters selling it to the gullible. The first person to jump from the bridge was a swimming instructor. Robert Odlum leaped off of the bridge on May 19, 1885. To lower the impact, he held one arm above his head and the other pressed to his side. Odlum survived the plunge but later died of internal bleeding. On July 23, 1886, Steve Brodie announced that he had survived a jump from the bridge. Several friends confirmed his story and told reporters how the crew of a passing barge plucked him out of the water. No one else besides Brodie's friends, however, had witnessed his leap. Most people believed that a dummy had been dropped from the bridge and that Brodie merely swam out from the shore. Police jailed him briefly, and a city ordinance outlawed jumping from the bridge. After Brodie was released, he opened a saloon that became popular with tourists. In 1884, Brodie starred in a hit Broadway play, *On the Bowery;* thousands flocked to the theater to see him reenact his leap from the bridge.

During the next few years, many others jumped from the bridge. Larry Donovan made the first confirmed successful leap. A worker who was painting the bridge survived an accidental

When the bridge was officially opened to the public, all types of people traveled across it *(above)*. Whether on foot, in carriages, or in wagons, many were determined to see the new structure and the panoramic view of the harbor it provided. The massive throngs of visitors were initially unregulated, which sometimes resulted in disaster.

fall. A deadly leap in 1892 is believed to be the first suicide jump from the bridge. By the turn of the century, the jumping fad had run its course.

When the Brooklyn Bridge opened in 1883, its towers were the tallest structures in North America. It was the last large bridge in North America to have stone towers; steel had become the foremost bridge-building material. Builders also used steel to construct tall buildings. New York's 612-foot (187-m) Singer Building was completed in 1908. Five years later, the city's 792-foot (241-m) Woolworth Building reached even higher. By the early 1920s, more than 400 steel skyscrapers in New York soared above the Brooklyn Bridge. All of these tall buildings lowered the impact of the Brooklyn Bridge on the city's skyline. The bridge, however, endured an as icon of the city.

During the next 50 years, three more bridges joined the Brooklyn Bridge on the East River. The Williamsburg Bridge was built upstream in 1903. Built 4 feet (1.2 m) longer than the Brooklyn Bridge, it took over as the world's longest suspension bridge. The Williamsburg Bridge was built entirely of steel, including its towers. The Roebling Wire Company used its wire to make the bridge's cables. The Manhattan Bridge was opened in 1901, and the Queensborough Bridge followed eight years later. On the other side of Manhattan, the George Washington Bridge opened in 1931. Spanning the Hudson River and connecting Manhattan to New Jersey, it features a span that is twice as long as the Brooklyn Bridge's.

In 1933, New York City planned to celebrate the fiftieth anniversary of the Brooklyn Bridge. A team of engineers was hired to examine the bridge and found no problems—they only recommended that it be painted. The fiftieth-anniversary festivities would not be as grand as the 1883 opening-day celebrations. In October 1929, a panic in the financial markets had triggered a severe economic crisis. This crisis became known as the Great Depression. The winter of 1932–1933 turned out to be the lowest point in the Depression. That winter, more than one-fourth of U.S. workers were unemployed, and the banking system seemed on the verge of collapse.

Despite the nation's hardships, the celebration of the Brooklyn Bridge's fiftieth year focused on the achievements of its construction. The *Brooklyn Eagle* published a supplement to commemorate the bridge. None of the celebration's speakers mentioned the current troubles. Instead, they focused on the bridge as a story of success and progress.

THE ROEBLINGS

After Washington Roebling resigned as chief engineer, he and Emily spent four years living in Troy, New York. Washington's health slowly improved, and the couple moved back to Trenton and built a house. The house featured a large stained-glass window that depicted the Brooklyn Bridge. Emily later studied law at New York University and traveled in Europe, while Washington busied himself with various scientific pursuits. He collected minerals and enjoyed bird-watching and astronomy. He and Emily would occasionally travel to New York and walk across the Brooklyn Bridge. No one ever recognized them.

Emily died of stomach cancer on February 28, 1903. Washington turned his energy to business; he made money in the stock market and bought back an interest in the family wire business. He soon became a wealthy man. The demand for wire had skyrocketed—it was needed for telegraph and electrical wires, bridge cables, oil rigs, and even elevators. His wealth would later be estimated at $29 million.

Washington married again in 1908. Despite his many years of poor health, Roebling outlived his younger brothers and several of his nephews. At age 84, he took full control of the family wire business again. Each workday, he got up, rode a trolley to the wire factory offices, and put in an eight-hour day. Nearly blind and deaf, his intellect remained sharp. He died, at age 89, on July 21, 1926. At his request, he was buried beside Emily in her family plot in Cold Spring, New York.

In 1944, the elevated trains that had earlier replaced the bridge's cable cars were taken out of service, and the terminals on each end of the bridge were demolished. Two years earlier, the ferries had stopped crossing the river. The age of the automobile had made these two forms of transportation outdated. The Brooklyn Bridge's deck was reconfigured for automotive traffic. With the train tracks removed, engineers added another lane for cars. The bridge reopened to pedestrians and vehicles in 1945. Five years later, the Brooklyn-Battery Tunnel opened downriver. Still one on the world's largest tunnels, it provided another way for automobiles to travel between Brooklyn and Manhattan.

The increased automobile traffic began to place too much stress on the bridge. In 1950, the bridge's chief engineer, David Steinman, made some changes to the bridge. He strengthened the roadway so it could stand up to heavy traffic and encased the outside roadways with steel girders. The renovations sparked controversy. *Architectural Forum* magazine published an editorial titled "What Happened to Brooklyn Bridge?" asserting that Steinman's alterations had ruined "what was most appealing in it. "The alterations had destroyed the bridge's graceful lines and obstructed the views from the pedestrian promenade. The magazine claimed that the bridge had lost its "old soaring magic."

In 1964, the Brooklyn Bridge was declared a National Historic Landmark. In 1983, thousands turned out for the bridge's one-hundredth anniversary. Today, nearly 150,000 vehicles cross the bridge every day. New Yorkers and visitors from around the country and around the world still stroll its promenade. About 30 workers take care of the bridge, and crews repaint it approximately every five years. The city's bridges department has stated that it requires less maintenance than any of New York's other major bridges.

CHAPTER 6

The Bridge, Then and Now

T he Brooklyn Bridge is part of the United States' national heritage. It has had an enormous impact on the economic and social life of New York City and the country. In his opening-day speech, Brooklyn mayor Seth Low called the bridge "an American triumph. American genius designed it, American skill built it, and American workshops made it. . . . Courage, enterprise, skill, faith, endurance—these are the qualities that have made the great Bridge." On the most basic level, the bridge did what it was supposed to do. It provided a much-needed transportation route between Manhattan and Brooklyn. It put Brooklyn on the map. It sparked economic and population growth in both cities.

The bridge was the most amazing engineering feat of its era. Everything about it was a marvel: its size, its location, and its design. In 1883, a writer for *Harper's Weekly* magazine predicted, "It so happens that the work which is likely to be our most durable monument and to convey some knowledge of us to

After the opening ceremonies and the public's initial reaction to New York City's newest structure, the Brooklyn Bridge *(above)* continued to maintain its popularity. Artists, writers, and photographers drew inspiration from the bridge and incorporated it into their work. The bridge has become one of the most photographed landmarks in New York City and is frequently used in popular films.

the most remote posterity is a work of bare utility, not a shrine, not a fortress, not a palace, but a bridge." In Ken Burns's documentary film *The Brooklyn Bridge* (1981), playwright Arthur Miller calls the bridge "steel poetry." In the same film, writer David McCullough says, "I think the bridge makes one glad to be alive. I think it makes you glad that you're part of the human community, that you're part of a species that could create such a structure."

THE CULTURAL CONNECTION

In addition to its physical impact, the Brooklyn Bridge also has had an enduring effect on the human imagination. The bridge is a vital part of New York City and the Manhattan skyline. It is difficult to imagine the city without it. Like the Statue of Liberty and the Empire State Building, the bridge has become an icon of New

BUILDING AMERICA NOW

HOOVER DAM BYPASS

The 2,000-foot (609-m) Colorado River Bridge will span the Colorado River about 1,600 feet (490 m) south of Hoover Dam. It will connect Arizona and Nevada, allowing traffic to bypass the roadway over the Hoover Dam. The new bridge was proposed as a solution to several problems caused by Hoover Dam's roadway. The road that crosses the Hoover Dam, U.S. 93, is the only major roadway in the area. As it approaches the Hoover Dam, the road is narrow, steep, and curvy. Low speed limits in this section cause traffic slowdowns. Pedestrians viewing the Hoover Dam often crowd the roadway at the top of the dam. A hazardous-materials spill or an explosion on top of the dam could damage it. Transportation officials expect traffic on U.S. 93 to grow rapidly in the future.

Construction on the Colorado River Bridge began in 2005, and the bridge is scheduled to open in 2010. It will be the first concrete-steel composite arch bridge in the United States. Concrete piers and a concrete arch will hold up a lighter steel upper structure. This hybrid design will make it easier to build the bridge over the 840-foot-deep (256-m) Black Canyon gorge. The design also allows the bridge to be built quickly and at a lower cost. Concrete piers and arches can be installed soon after the foundations are ready.

York City. On a larger scale, it is a symbol of American know-how and can-do attitude.

Since its opening, the Brooklyn Bridge has appeared in countless advertisements, songs, films, paintings, photographs, and literary works. The bridge has been featured in ads that sell everything from sodas and sewing machines to mobile phones and Internet services. It has appeared in many songs, such as

THE BROOKLYN BRIDGE BY THE NUMBERS

GENERAL

Years of construction	1869–1883
Total length of bridge	3,455.5 feet (1,053 m)
Length of land spans (each side)	930 feet (283 m)
Length of river span	1,595.5 feet (486 m)
Length of New York approach (road)	971 feet (296 m)
Length of Brooklyn approach (road)	930 feet (283 m)
Width of bridge deck	85 feet (26 m)
Total weight of the bridge (excluding masonry)	14,680 tons (13,318 metric tons)
Total weight of suspended structure (anchorage to anchorage)	6,620 tons (6,006 metric tons)

TOWERS

Height of each tower (above high water)	276.5 feet (84.2 m)
Width of opening through towers	33.75 feet (10.3 m)
Depth of New York foundation (below high water)	78.5 feet (23.9 m)
Depth of Brooklyn foundation (below high water)	44.5 feet (13.6 m)

the 1883 hit "Strolling on the Brooklyn Bridge," and jazz master Sonny Rollins's 1962 album, *The Bridge.*

Artists, photographers, and filmmakers have long been drawn to the bridge. Artists as diverse as Childe Hassam, Georgia O'Keefe, and Andy Warhol have expressed their visions of the bridge. In his oil painting *A Winter Day on Brooklyn Bridge* (1892), Childe Hassam concentrates on the experience of crossing

Size of New York caisson	172 feet × 102 feet × 14.5 feet (52.4 m × 31 m × 4.4 m)
Size of Brooklyn caisson	168 feet × 102 feet × 14.5 feet (51 m × 31 m × 4.4 m)

CABLES

Number of main cables	4
Diameter of each cable	15.75 inches (40 cm)
Length of each cable	3,578.5 feet (1,090.7 m)
Number of wires in each cable	5,434
Length of wire in each cable	3,515 miles (5,657 km)
Weight of each cable	1,732,086 pounds (785,653 kg)
Number of suspenders	1,176

ANCHORAGES

Weight of each anchorage	60,000 tons (54,432 metric tons)
Total number of anchor plates	8
Weight of each anchor plate	23 tons (20.9 metric tons)

the bridge. (Interestingly, he omits most of the bridge's cables.) John Marin's drawing *Brooklyn Bridge, 1913* shows a more modernist view of the bridge, full of energy and motion. *Sur Brooklyn Bridge* (*On Brooklyn Bridge*), a 1917 oil painting by Albert Gleizes, portrays a similar burst of energy—whether the painting evokes excitement or chaos is left up to the viewer. Louis Lozowick's oil painting *New York, 1925* shows the Brooklyn Bridge as part of New York's modern, geometric skyline. In the 1940s and 1950s, such noted artists as Georgia O'Keefe, Franz Kline,

A TRIBUTE IN SONG

Some love to ramble in the park
When sunset hours are near.
Some like to linger after dark,
When stars are shining clear.

But give to me the pathway sweet
Above the waters blue.
It's on the Brooklyn Bridge we meet
I and my darling true.

Strolling over the Brooklyn Bridge
Drowsy hours go by.
Whispering words of fond delight
Beneath the starry sky.
Happy as the dancing waves
Hearts are lost and won.
We fondly stray
With hearts so gay,
Upon the Brooklyn Bridge.

—from "Strolling on the Brooklyn Bridge" (1883);
words by George Cooper; music by J.P. Skelly

and Ellsworth Kelly produced works that focused on the bridge's geometry. Paintings by Joseph Stella and Yee Gee used the bridge as a backdrop for darker, more threatening portraits of the city.

Like painters, photographers have long been drawn to the Brooklyn Bridge. The Library of Congress has more photographs of the Brooklyn Bridge than any other human-made structure. In 1876, Joshua Beal climbed to the top of the bridge's Brooklyn tower and took a series of photographs of lower New York. The photographs were widely published and came to symbolize the promise of a bright future. The harbor was full of ships. The docks were full of goods being imported and exported. The Western Union and post office demonstrated the rise of faster and better communications. Later photographers focused on the bridge's graceful geometry. In the 1910s, Karl Struss used the bridge's cables to frame views of New York. Many others followed his lead. In the 1920s and 1930s, Walker Evans photographed many aspects of the bridge. George Hall and Alfred Stieglitz created other well-known photographs of the bridge.

Filmmakers have long used the Brooklyn Bridge as a setting for their movies. Thomas Edison made one of the first motion pictures of the Brooklyn Bridge. In 1899, he placed his camera on one of the bridge's elevated trains; it took pictures as the train traveled from Brooklyn to Manhattan. The bridge has appeared in *Planet of the Apes* (1968), *Saturday Night Fever* (1977), *Night on Earth* (1991), *The Fantastic Four* (2005), *Superman Returns* (2006), and many other films. The bridge is also featured in many television shows, music videos, and video games.

Many poets and writers have written about the bridge as well. Although poet Walt Whitman was a constant champion of Brooklyn and New York, he never wrote a poem about the bridge. The best-known poem about the bridge is Hart Crane's long, epic poem *The Bridge* (1930). The poem "To Brooklyn Bridge" serves as the prelude to the longer poem and uses the bridge to look closely at human aspirations and achievements. Coincidentally, Crane lived in an apartment in the same Brooklyn Heights house that the Roeblings owned during construction of the bridge. In a letter to his family, Crane describes the view from his window, "[U]p at the right, the Brooklyn Bridge, the most superb piece of construction in the modern world, I'm sure, with strings of light crossing it like glow worms as the Ls [elevated trains] pass each other coming and going." Without knowing it, Crane was looking out of the same window that Washington Roebling used to watch the progress of the bridge's construction. Every June, New York City's Poets House hosts the Brooklyn Bridge Poetry Walk. This event, which started in 1996, features a walk across the bridge with stops for readings, as well as a poetry reading at the Fulton Ferry Landing in Brooklyn.

Although the bridge had debuted as the longest suspension bridge in the world, new feats of engineering have developed longer, more complex structures. The Brooklyn Bridge, however, continues to be one of the most famous bridges in the world. It has become an enduring symbol of New York and the daring and imagination of its inhabitants.

Writers have also featured the Brooklyn Bridge in many novels. The bridge appears in John Dos Passos's *Manhattan Transfer* (1925), Thomas Wolfe's *The Web and the Rock* (1939) and *You Can't Go Home Again* (1940), Henry Miller's *Tropic of Capricorn* (1939), and Richard Crabbe's mystery novel *Suspension* (2000). In Betty Smith's *A Tree Grows in Brooklyn* (1943), a soldier recalls, "I thought if I ever got to New York, I'd like to walk across the Brooklyn Bridge." Beat writers Jack Kerouac and Allen Ginsberg often walked on the bridge, discussing literature and life. In her young-adult novel *The Spider of Brooklyn Heights* (1967), Nancy Veglahn used Washington Roebling's letters and journals and other primary sources to write a realistic historical novel about the building of the Brooklyn Bridge.

THE BRIDGE'S PROMISE

The Brooklyn Bridge remains the most popular bridge in New York. The bridge has changed over the years. Automobiles and trucks now cross it instead of horses and carriages, and many skyscrapers rise high above it. Its Gothic arches, however, have endured. Today, more than 160,000 people cross the bridge every day.

In his original 1867 plans for the Brooklyn Bridge, John Roebling stated his lofty goals:

> The completed work, when constructed in accordance with my designs, will not only be the greatest bridge in existence, but it will be the greatest engineering work of the continent, and of the age. Its most conspicuous features, the great towers, will serve as landmarks to the adjoining cities, and they will be entitled to be ranked as national monuments. As a great work of art, and as a successful specimen of advanced bridge engineering, this structure will forever testify to the energy, enterprise and wealth of that community which shall secure its erection.

More than 140 years later, the Brooklyn Bridge continues to fulfill his hope.

1802   A petition submitted to the New York State legislature proposes constructing a bridge across the East River.

1857   The New York State legislature considers a bill to build a suspension bridge over the East River; no action is taken.

1866   The New York State legislature passes a bill to construct a bridge over the East River.

1867   The New York Bridge Company is incorporated in April; it appoints John A. Roebling as chief engineer in May.

TIMELINE

1866
The New York State legislature passes a bill to construct a bridge over the East River.

1802
A petition submitted to the New York State legislature proposes constructing a bridge across the East River.

1802 — **1869**

1867
The New York Bridge Company appoints John A. Roebling as chief engineer.

1869
John Roebling dies; Washington Roebling is appointed chief engineer.

1869 Monies to build the bridge are raised and government approval is granted; John Roebling dies; Washington Roebling is appointed chief engineer.

1870 *January* Work on the bridge begins.

May Work inside the Brooklyn caisson begins.

December Fire is discovered in the Brooklyn caisson; Roebling is stricken with caisson disease.

1871 The Brooklyn tower foundation is completed; work inside the New York caisson begins.

1872 *May* Roebling stops the New York caisson's descent.

July The New York tower foundation is completed.

1875 *June* The Brooklyn tower is completed.

November The Brooklyn anchorage is completed.

1876
August The first wire for cable is stretched across the river; E.F. Farrington makes the first crossing.

1883
May 24 The bridge opens.

1870 ——————— 1983

1870
January Work on the bridge begins.
December Roebling is stricken with caisson disease.

1983
The bridge's one-hundredth anniversary is celebrated.

1876   *July*   The New York tower and anchorage are completed.

August   The first wire for cable is stretched across the river; E.F. Farrington makes the first crossing.

1877   *June*   Cable-making begins; a temporary footbridge between the towers is built; a scandal over substandard wire begins.

1878   *October*   The cables are completed.

1881   *December*   The structure for the bridge deck is completed.

1883   *April*   The trusswork and promenade are completed.

May 24   The bridge opens.

1933   The bridge's fiftieth anniversary is celebrated.

1944   Bridge renovations are made.

1983   The bridge's one-hundredth anniversary is celebrated.

2001   *September 11*   Thousands of people cross the bridge on foot when public transportation is suspended because of terrorist attacks on the World Trade Center.

GLOSSARY

air spinning   A method of making the cables for a suspension bridge by passing individual wires back and forth across the entire span until the suspension cable is built up to the correct size.

anchorages   The onshore support structures for holding the cable ends of a suspension bridge.

aqueduct   A structure that carries a canal over a river.

bedrock   The solid rock layer beneath the silt and sand of a river.

bends   *See* caisson disease.

caisson   A structure used for building bridge foundations underwater; it has a working chamber filled with compressed air.

caisson disease   A disease caused by bubbles of nitrogen in the blood; affects divers and workers working in caissons who come out of the airlock too quickly.

ceck   The top side of a beam, box girder, or truss that forms the running surface for vehicles and pedestrians.

cement   A powder that, when mixed with water, binds a stone-and-sand mixture into a strong concrete when dried.

civil engineering   The branch of engineering concerned with the design and construction of public works, such as dams, highways, and bridges.

concrete   A mixture of sand, stone, and water bound by cement, which hardens into a rocklike material.

eyebar   Pieces of metal that have holes in each end.

galvanization   The process in which steel, iron, and other metals are coated with the metal zinc to prevent rust.

pier   The support of a bridge deck span that is located in the water; also a general term for the base or foundation of a bridge.

stays   Wires that run from a bridge's towers to its deck and make the bridge more stable.

107

steel   An alloy of iron that has more carbon than wrought iron and less carbon than cast iron; combines the tensile strength of wrought iron and the compressive strength of cast iron.

stocks   Titles to a share in the ownership of a company.

suspenders   The wires or bars with which the deck is hung from the cables in a suspension bridge.

suspension bridge   A bridge whose deck is supported by large cables or chains draped from towers and secured on anchorages.

tower   The vertical support structure of a suspension bridge from which the cables are hung.

truss   A section of a bridge's metal framework that is often used to make a deck.

viaduct   A bridge that carries a road or a railroad.

BIBLIOGRAPHY

Bennett, David. *The Creation of Bridges*. Edison, N.J.: Chartwell, 1999.

Brown, David. *Bridges: Three Thousand Years of Defying Nature*. Richmond Hill, Ontario, Canada: Firefly, 2005.

Condit, Carl W. *American Building Art: The Nineteenth Century*. New York: Oxford University Press, 1960.

Ellis, Edward Robb. *The Epic of New York City*. New York: Carroll & Graf, 2001.

Haw, Richard. *The Brooklyn Bridge: A Cultural History*. New Brunswick, N.J.: Rutgers University Press, 2005.

McCullough, David. *The Great Bridge*. New York: Simon and Schuster, 2001.

Plowden, David. *Bridges: The Spans of North America*. New York: Viking, 1974.

Reiter, Sharon. *The Bridges of New York*. Mineola, N.Y.: Dover, 2000 (reprint of New York: Quadrant, 1977).

Sassi Perino, Angia. *Bridges: Triumphs of Engineering*. New York: Barnes and Noble, 2004.

Sayenga, Donald, *Ellet and Roebling*. York, Penn.: American Canal and Transportation Center, 1983.

Spangenburg, Ray, and Diane K. Moser. *The Story of America's Bridges*. New York: Facts On File, 1991.

Steinman, D.B. *The Builders of the Bridge: The Story of John Roebling and His Son*. New York: Harcourt Brace and Co., 1945.

FURTHER RESOURCES

BOOKS

Bennett, David. *The Creation of Bridges*. Edison, N.J.: Chartwell, 1999.

Dupré, Judith. *Bridges: A History of the World's Most Famous and Important Spans*. New York: Black Dog & Leventhal, 1997.

Johnson, Stephen. *Encyclopedia of Bridges and Tunnels*. New York: Facts On File, 2002.

Ricciuti, Edward. *America's Top Ten Bridges*. Woodbridge, Conn.: Blackbirch, 1998.

Shapiro, Mary. *A Picture History of the Brooklyn Bridge*. Mineola, N.Y.: Dover, 1983.

Spangenburg, Ray, and Diane K. Moser. *The Story of America's Bridges*. New York: Facts On File, 1991.

Veglahn, Nancy. *The Spider of Brooklyn Heights*. New York: Encore, 1967.

Weiner, Vicki. *The Brooklyn Bridge: New York City's Graceful Connection*. Danbury, Conn.: Children's Press, 2003.

DVD

Brooklyn Bridge: A Film by Ken Burns. Alexandria, V.A.: PBS DVD Video, 2002.

WEB SITES

Brooklyn Eagle articles on the bridge's opening
http://eagle.brooklynpubliclibrary.org/Archive/skins/BE/NavigationSites/what.htm

Information on Emily Roebling
http://www.pausingtoremember.net/Emily's_Bridge.html

Ken Burns's Brooklyn Bridge documentary
http://www.pbs.org/kenburns/brooklynbridge/

PBS's Wonders of the World database
http://www.pbs.org/wgbh/buildingbig/wonder/structure/
    brooklyn.html

PICTURE CREDITS

INDEX

G.S. PRENTZAS is an editor and writer who lives in New York. He has written more than 20 books for young readers, including *Gideon v. Wainwright* in Chelsea House's GREAT SUPREME COURT DECISIONS series, *Thurgood Marshall: Champion of Justice*, and *Tribal Law*. He is a former resident of Brooklyn.